EDUCATION AND YOUTH EMPLOYMENT IN GREAT BRITAIN

Stuart Maclure

**CARNEGIE COUNCIL ON POLICY STUDIES
IN HIGHER EDUCATION**

EDUCATION AND YOUTH EMPLOYMENT IN GREAT BRITAIN
by Stuart Maclure

*The Carnegie Council on Policy Studies in Higher Education, 2150 Shattuck Avenue,
Berkeley, California 94704, has sponsored publication of this report as part of a continuing effort to obtain and present significant information for public discussion. The
views expressed are those of the author.*

Library of Congress Catalog Card Number LC 78-75167

International Standard Book Number ISBN 0-931050-08-1

Manufactured in the United States of America

Education and Youth Employment in Contemporary Societies

A Series of Special Studies

BELGIUM
Henri Janne

GREAT BRITAIN
Stuart Maclure

JAPAN
Hidetoshi Kato

MEXICO AND SOUTH ASIA
Alberto Hernández Medina, Carlos Muñoz Izquierdo/Manzoor Ahmed

POLAND
Barbara Liberska

SWEDEN AND DENMARK
Gösta Rehn, K. Helveg Petersen

FEDERAL REPUBLIC OF GERMANY
Klaus von Dohnanyi

These publications are available from the Carnegie Council on Policy Studies in Higher Education, 2150 Shattuck Avenue, Berkeley, California 94704.

Contents

*Local government and other public service
interventions • Government interventions
beyond 1977 • Interventions in the labor
market for those aged 19 to 25*

Foreword

This is one of seven publications presenting studies commissioned by the Carnegie Council on Policy Studies in Higher Education as a means of providing a global perspective for education and youth employment in contemporary societies. The remaining publications will be concerned with education and youth employment in Belgium, by Henri Janne; Japan, by Hidetoshi Kato; Mexico and South Asia, by Alberto Hernández Medina and Carlos Munoz Izquierdo and Manzoor Ahmed, respectively; Poland, by Barbara Liberska; Sweden and Denmark, by Gösta Rehn and K. Helveg Petersen, respectively; and The Federal Republic of Germany by Klaus von Dohnanyi. Margaret S. Gordon, associate director of the Carnegie Council on Policy Studies in Higher Education, is the general editor of the series. To the authors of these studies, and to Stuart Maclure, whose work appears in this volume, we express our deep appreciation.

The German Marshall Fund generously provided support for two international conferences on education and youth employment which were attended by several of the authors of studies for this series and which have contributed significantly to the Council's deliberations on this subject. The International Council for Educational Development, under the direction of James A. Perkins, arranged for the participation of the essayists in this project. We acknowledge these contributions with profound thanks.

We also wish to extend our thanks to Mary Purnell Frederick and Diana Lorentz for their editorial contributions, and Sylvia Zuck for coordinating manuscript preparation.

CLARK KERR
Chairman,
Carnegie Council on Policy Studies
in Higher Education

1

Introduction

This study arises from the difficulties that young people are presently experiencing in negotiating transitions from school to work and from youth to adulthood. Put baldly like that, it sounds like the patronizing concern of middle age. Youth tend to be seen by their patronizing elders in terms of "problems"— as if the very condition of being young needs specific and unpleasant remedies. However, this is not just a routine reflection of the anxieties of the middle-aged middle class. The difficulties young people face with regard to employment are apparent for all to see. In Britain, unemployment is at a postwar peak, and there has been a disproportionately large increase in the number of young unemployed people. In particular, school leavers have had difficulty in finding jobs: unemployment among 16- and 17-year-olds rose by 120 percent between January 1972 and January 1977, by which time these youth represented 9 percent of all unemployed (see Chapter 2). Furthermore, the present unemployment figures must be seen against a demographic trend that will increase the size of the relevant age groups over the next five to ten years and other social trends, including the return of more women to the work force, some of whom will be competing for jobs with teenagers and young adults.

In the light of all this, forecasts project a continuing high level of youth unemployment, and the conventional view is that full employment can be restored only if economic growth can

Note. My thanks are due to Lois Rodgers and Mark Jackson, who have assisted me throughout this project. The final product is, of course, my responsibility.

be sustained over a period at a higher level (5 percent) than has proved possible until now.

Youth unemployment has become a major political concern for government. At a time when expenditures on most public services are closely scrutinized, funds have been freely available for special programs of job creation and industrial training for youth (see Chapter 5). In Britain, as in most developed Western countries, labor-market questions continue to receive high priority.

The rise in youth unemployment affects those in the ages between the mid-teens and mid-twenties—a decade in which boys and girls become men and women and move out of the world of school and childhood and into the world of work and adulthood. Finding a job and working is part of achieving full adult status. It is one way of establishing an identity, a definition by which one knows oneself and is known by others. If the passage from school to work is interrupted, a "backwash" effect interferes with the process. Youth unemployment introduces uncertainty at a critical stage of development. Just as one receives status by having a job, one is also stigmatized and separated from the rest of the working community by not having a job. This is true not only for those who leave school and enter a period of idleness or intermittent work but also for young adults who lose their jobs in their early twenties or whose chances of settling in to permanent employment after an experimental period of job changing and transience are unduly delayed. Unemployment is higher than average for the 20- to 24-year-olds as well as for the younger age groups.

Unemployment, then, is one cause of discontinuity and uncertainty for the young. Other factors that have complicated the process can be identified in education and industrial training. An ever-lengthening span of primary, secondary, and tertiary education has been a feature of all the developed countries. Britain has been slower than most countries to expand secondary and postsecondary education, but even in Britain, the proportion of youths staying in full-time education to 18, 21, and older has risen steadily, thereby raising the average age of entry into employment by nearly three years in the past 30 years. As education has come to absorb more and more of the first quarter-century of every man and woman's life, the young have been required to spend longer in the "limbo" between childhood and adulthood. A contradiction is obviously implicit in lengthening social adolescence when improved diet and physical surroundings have lowered the age of the onset of puberty. Education has also become more important in determining vocational opportunity. Entry into the labor market is linked to particular stages of education—to school examinations at 16 and 18, to university degrees and professional diplomas, and to vocational and technical training. The education system's function as a filter also shapes the self-image of potential adults, branding some as failures at an early age and marking others for success. Fortunately, there is no perfect correlation between education's assessment and that of the outside world, but there is enough correlation to make the system work and to have a dispiriting effect on the bottom third of the school population.

The 30 years of educational development since the end of the Second World War have widened educational opportunity and extended access at the upper levels but have not seriously altered the close links between educational success and social class (as we shall see in Chapter 4). The socially disadvantaged and some ethnic minority groups are strongly represented among the least successful sections of the school population and are most likely to be hostile to school and least equipped— psychologically as well as technically—for employment.

Industrial training in Britain is a responsibility of industry (see Chapter 3) and a great deal remains to be done to put it on a sound basis and to insulate the training function more effectively from fluctuations in economic conditions. But the basic structures of industrial training, like the traditional mechanisms of apprenticeship, interact with the trade unions and the system of industrial relations. The tasks of incorporating people leaving school and college into employment and equipping them with the changing skills of modern industry are caught up in the larger issues of the power of management and unions and the balance of interunion strength. The shortcomings of industrial relations in Britain, therefore, have their impact on the lives of young workers and their opportunities for job satisfaction.

Other factors that have affected youth employment have arisen from shifts in the balance of industrial activity. The long-run decline of employment in manufacturing has continued, with a corresponding increase in service jobs, many of them in the public sector. Different types of employment have meant different types of recruitment and different training and educational requirements. Some jobs have been automated, requiring less skill; at the same time, new openings for technicians have been created—not enough to offset increasing unemployment, but continuing to provide vacancies for men and women with certain skills. Much of the energy of the industrial training boards has gone into locating such imbalances and trying to eliminate them.

Alongside the changes that have arisen from technological advance and economic retreat have been those originating with social and fiscal policy. The growth of public-sector employment has resulted from political priorities of how national resources should be divided among public and private consumption, investment, and savings.

Changes in employment patterns have resulted in sharp differences in unemployment levels in various parts of the country. Southeast England has been more severely affected than less heavily industrialized East Anglia (see Figure 9 in Chapter 2). The reduction of employment in the London area has been accentuated by the movement of manufacturing out of the metropolis for planning reasons. The result has been an inner ring, where service jobs have not increased fast enough to fill the vacuum created by the exodus of manufacturing. High unemployment figures have resulted, particularly among young West Indians congregated in particular inner-London areas.

Changes in the structure of industry, in industrial relations, and in social policy have also been reflected in the wage structure and the economics of youth employment. Technological and organizational changes have altered the demand for different kinds of labor and different forms of skill. British politics since the mid-1960s have revolved in large measure around the power of the trade unions and the use of their bargaining power. Both political parties have looked at ways of curbing the unions. Sir Harold Wilson's Labor Government of 1966–1970 examined proposals for limiting union power but dropped them in the face of opposition. Mr. Edward Heath's Conservative Government of 1970–1974 brought in the Industrial Relations Act, which sought to impose a new legal framework on industrial relations. This, too, aroused the unremitting opposition of the unions. When attempts to enforce a wage policy broke down, a strike by the miners in direct opposition to the Parliament-backed policies of the Heath government precipitated the General Election of 1974 and a new majority in the House of Commons. The new Labor Government of 1974 was committed to the repeal of Conservative industrial-relations legislation and to the operation of a so-called social contract between government and unions which led in the fiscal year 1974–75 to a period of unparalleled wage inflation* and made the unions the effective arbiters of government economic policy until the summer of 1975.

The effect of this wage explosion in the two years that followed has been to increase sharply the earnings of the lower paid (including the young) relative to the rest of the labor force. The dominant figure on the trade union side has been Mr. Jack Jones, leader of the Transport and General Workers Union, the largest general union, whose members include a large number of lower-paid workers. The effect of these measures on those under 21 has been accentuated by the delayed consequences of lowering the legal age of majority to 18. With their freedom to alter pay rates limited by wage policy, the trade unions have turned their attention to fringe benefits and similar side issues. More and more settlements have provided for the payment of the full adult rate at 18 instead of 21, telescoping the period of

---

*This is not, of course, to say that the social contract was the only factor causing the inflation of 1974–75 or to exclude the oil price increase and the economic and monetary policies of the Heath government between 1970 and 1974. However, the social contract dominated political argument and influenced social and industrial policies affecting employment.

pay at lower rates for younger workers. Also, the raising of the school leaving age from 15 to 16 has had the effect of raising starting rates. In the same period also, early legislation on equal pay has begun to take effect, causing women's wage levels to rise faster than they would otherwise have done.

Along with increases in wage rates there have been steady increases in social payments—unemployment benefits that depend on contributions debited during employment and paid for in an initial period on an earnings-related basis. There are also supplementary benefits which are paid without any qualifying period of employment and other forms of compensation payable to workers who are laid off after a minimum period of employment with the same firm. These payments, like higher unemployment pay and supplementary benefits, are intended to cushion the effect of being put out of work. How far the cushion itself has raised the residual level of unemployment by extending the waiting period between jobs remains an open question. It was a deliberate aim of policy in the mid-1960s to increase unemployment benefits to facilitate what was then euphemistically called "redeployment" of labor—that is, the redistribution expected as part of any modernization process. It is certainly likely that the benefits have had some effect in increasing the number of young people registered as unemployed: whereas formerly youngsters leaving school might have been content to look around for some weeks before regarding themselves as unemployed, now immediate registration has prompt cash value.

British social policy has so far proved incapable of dealing with the anomalies that follow from income-related cash benefits, especially the so-called poverty trap where social benefits may actually exceed compensation for employment, resulting in a clear disincentive to work. For example, former university students and graduates of teacher-training colleges, because of generous social-welfare payments, can spend a longer time searching for openings in their preferred occupations. Jobs for teachers have been many fewer in number than the qualified candidates emerging from the colleges. There is evidence that many who have been unsuccessful in their quest for a teaching post have taken several months to become convinced that they must turn to something else and, for them, the difference between living on supplementary benefit and living on a student's maintenance grant is small. Nevertheless, improved social benefits are certainly a marginal factor in raising the level of unemployment.

A survey carried out by the Manpower Services Commission (MSC) in the winter of 1976–77 examined the attitudes of employers, unemployed young people, and young people generally. The results (MSC, 1977, p. 17) show that most unemployed young people "are actively seeking jobs; 40 percent of those interviewed had applied for more than six jobs, and very few had refused an offer of a job." There is no evidence that there are plenty of "dirty" jobs available which young white boys and girls reject as beneath them.

The survey showed that "about half the employers believe that the caliber of young people has deteriorated over the past five years in terms of their motivation and basic education" but that they expected to employ the same proportion of young people in the future as in the past. In most cases, young people were seen to be in competition for employment with other age groups. Only in entry to skill training did recognizable "young people jobs" exist. Employers complained about the attitude, personality, appearance, manners, and inadequate knowledge of the "three R's" of the young people they interviewed for jobs. Even if this release of pent-up criticism of youthful mores and of modern education cannot be taken at face value, the criticism does relate to more serious doubts about inadequate links between school and work and the suspicion that the tradition of English liberal education (not to mention the tendencies of radical members of the teaching profession) is hostile to industry and industrial employment.

Some 14 percent of unemployed young people, according to the survey, "reported that their fathers were also unemployed; 22 percent that brothers or sisters were unemployed; and 19 percent were living in households where no one was in full-time employment." The survey did not collect information on other forms of social disadvantage, but families with several members out of work would be expected to suffer other social misfortunes such as overcrowded housing, poor health, and a lifetime of poverty.

Another social policy that has had an important bearing on youth concerns the protection of the employment of those already working. Employees have been given legal protection against unfair dismissal as well as compensation if they are laid off. The new laws back up the already strong trade unions and have the effect of raising the liabilities of employers who take on staff. This is one of several measures that may have increased the cost of employment; it is likely that if any economies of labor are needed, they will be achieved by stopping recruitment rather than by letting older workers go. There are good reasons for trade unions to favor such legislation, just as there are good reasons why those who have clambered aboard the rescue ship should kick down the ladder before it becomes overburdened. But the effect, like the operation of the sacred principle of "last in, first out," now also underwritten by case law, has the effect to make sure that young people are disproportionately likely to appear in the unemployment statistics.

Such inflexibilities as these need to be seen against the background of a lengthy period of very low postwar unemployment to the early 1970s and an industrial economy with low productivity per worker, reflecting, in many industries, overhiring as a result of union strength and management weakness. Both inflexibility and low productivity can be linked to the structure of trade-union organization—the continued strength of craft-based unions and the measures taken to maintain sharp demarcation among skills—and the paradoxical strength of unions in declining industries (for instance, dock workers), where unions have striven with some success to gain the recognition of workers' rights to obsolescent jobs. The printing industry is another where a strong rear-guard action is being fought against technological redundancy.

To sum up, therefore, the present state of youth unemployment is connected to three sets of cyclical and structural factors:

Cyclical and demographic factors. Youth unemployment is high because all unemployment is high and because the age groups concerned are large. Given an upturn in the level of the economy, the number of people without work would be much reduced. By the same token, the macroeconomic policies required to put things right are the same for younger and older alike.

"Full employment" is a commitment of all the major political parties, and most discussion has been based on the hypothesis that cyclical factors are dominant—that if only the management of the economy, domestic and international, could be set right, youth unemployment would cease to be a problem. However, this argument must be seen in the context of steadily rising unemployment over the past two decades. The residual level of unemployment at the high point of the economic cycle has risen, and as a result there is little agreement on the definition of "full employment." (See Worswick, 1976, for a comprehensive discussion.)

Demographic trends indicate that the numbers in the 16–24 age group will go on rising into the mid-1980s and then decline through the 1990s. In the long term, therefore, the demographic trend will reduce pressure on employment for younger people; in the short term, it will accentuate it (Figure 1).

Technological and structural factors. Another set of developments bearing on the employment of young people relates to changes in the industrial process—changes that lead to the "de-skilling" of some jobs and the upgrading of other (perhaps fewer) jobs, thus affecting the range of training positions traditionally provided for young people. The balance between the manufacturing and service sectors changes. Old industries become obsolete and new ones (hopefully) take their place, changing the demand for particular skills and kinds of labor. International competition causes one industry to contract,

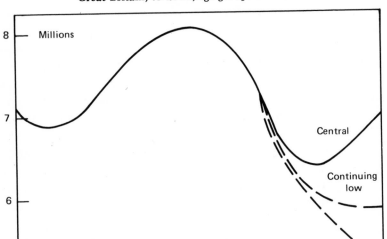

Figure 1. 1974-based population projection for Great Britain, to 2001, age group: 16 to 24

Source: Central Policy Review Staff, 1977.

another to expand, and in the process takes employment away or gives it to particular groups of workers.

Social policy changes. Youth employment is also affected by social policies adopted by governments and by influence exerted by political parties and pressure groups, such as employers' organizations and trade unions. Wage policy, job protection legislation, women's rights, social security payments, trade-union power, taxation policy—in all these areas action has been taken that has affected the cost of employment and the flexibility of the labor market and, directly or indirectly, altered the relative chances of employment among different groups of potential employees. The social policy measures include various temporary programs (described in Chapter 5) that have alleviated youth unemployment and, by creating or subsidizing jobs for particular categories of workers, have sought to counteract the pressures arising from other policies.

The way in which these structural, demographic, technological, commercial, social, and political factors interact remains a matter of lively controversy. What is clear is that the pressures that have built up behind policies indirectly inimical to youth employment show no signs of abating, and there is little reason to doubt that unemployment among young workers will continue at a high level over the next five years. True, there is a widespread conviction that if the economy were to bounce back (aided by the temporary boost to the balance of payments provided by North Sea oil), there would be an immediate improvement in employment among the young. But to some extent this belief is based on a possibly correct but unflattering estimate of the acumen of British management; against it must be set the suggestion that there is scope for a considerable improvement in output within present manning levels and without any substantial increase in recruitment of young people.

The present industrial strategy—adopted by government, industry, and the trade unions in 1975—is linked to increasing the resources of manufacturing industry and export-oriented commerce. It assumes that the expansion of the public-service sector will be restrained to allow the extra resources to flow into export-led growth and therefore does not envisage any marked expansion in national and local government service which, until recently, has absorbed increasing numbers of workers.

The growth of youth unemployment in Britain—essentially a recent phenomenon which has appeared in the wake of overall economic recession—is consistent with a larger scenario of post-industrial development. One component of this scenario is the steadily expanding period of secondary and postsecondary education, causing a postponement of entry into the primary labor market until the early or middle twenties and lengthening the period spent in higher and vocational education, temporary employment, and reliance on social benefits. This implies a yet longer period of socially imposed "youth," a social adolescence to be served as probation before gaining access to the settled realm of employment and to penetrating the defenses that adult workers erect to protect themselves from the insecurity of rapid industrial change. The British experience, however, is not entirely consistent with such a scenario. Britain still has a long way to go in the process of industrial development. Though teenage unemployment (for short periods) is a cause of worry, most youth under 18, and the very great majority of those aged 16 to 25, work most of the time. The education system is developing slowly. It loses most young people well before the end of secondary school, and only a small fraction of the age group continues into full-time postsecondary education. However, the development of a large program of work experience—offering an alternative to unemployment for a large proportion of young people who would otherwise find themselves on relief (see Chapter 5)—comes at a time when questions about the appropriate form of secondary education for an industrial society are being asked with new persistence.

The work-experience program (which will include elements of education and industrial training) is an attempt to rationalize the ad hoc schemes that have developed since 1975 and been financed on a short-term basis. What is now proposed still is not necessarily a "permanent" program but a countercyclical instrument to expand or contract according to the state of the economy and the level of employment. And, as the official forecasts assume high youth unemployment to 1981 at least, the work-experience program will tend to develop a life of its own and have a direct impact on other public provisions for the 16 to 18 age groups in schools and colleges of further education.

Most obviously, the work-experience program is likely to affect teenage economics: each boy or girl accepted into a work-experience scheme will qualify at once for £18 a week—considerably more than the educational maintenance allowances offered by education authorities to children from poor families who remain in school or college beyond the age of 16. Concern has been expressed by the Manpower Services Commission and the Department of Education and Science about the difficulties this may cause when children who take advantage of a work-experience opportunity later recognize the need to return to full-time education. Widespread development of work-experience schemes could lead to recurrent education and easier two-way transit between the worlds of work and education, but not unless this financial barrier can be bridged.

When all is said and done, the main determinant of the level of unemployment will still be macroeconomic policies constrained by cyclical economic fluctuations, internal politics, the need to curb inflation, pressures on the balance of payments, and the terms of trade. But educational policies—especially industrial training policies—can marginally increase the government's capacity to run the economy at a high level by ensuring that the right skills are available in adequate numbers and by eliminating shortages of specific skills. Any policy for youth unemployment must include a plan to improve the quality of the labor force and use some of the slack caused by unemployment to train and retrain workers for skills that are or will be in high demand.

Attempts are being made to do this in Britain through the Manpower Services Commission and the Training Services Agency, but nothing less than a transformation of the attitudes of employers and trade unionists toward training is needed. Along with this goes the need for a much closer relationship between education and industry.

Officials are depending greatly on the industry curriculum development project being undertaken by the Schools Council in cooperation with both the Trades Union Congress and the Confederation of British Industries. This project will generate teaching materials for social studies in secondary schools aimed at increased knowledge of industry and greater realism on the part of the schools about the world of work. But it would be fantasy to suppose that the study of industrial history will necessarily make young people more willing to accept the disciplines and values of the capitalist economy or improve their attitudes toward the production line.

The measures now proposed—expansion of career education, work experience in the later years of school, introduction of teachers to industrial matters through in-service training, and

large-scale development of work-experience schemes for the 16-
to 18-year-olds—eventually raise the key British questions about
growing up in a rather unsuccessful industrial nation in the last
quarter of the twentieth century. They also raise questions
about the quality of life in the factory and in the city; about
job enrichment (which is more talked about than pursued) and
job impoverishment (a continuing aspect of the division of labor
in the not-very-assiduous pursuit of productive efficiency);
about whether rising standards of material well-being outside
work can compensate for a life of boredom and frustration at
the work place; and whether economic growth can take place
quickly enough to keep pace with the rise in consumer aspirations. Anecdotal evidence of alienation among the young is not
difficult to assemble: it can be found in violence and crime,
football hooliganism and mindless vandalism, drug and alcohol
abuse, poor attitudes to school and later to work. But these are
clearly young people with a lot to be alienated against. Even the
use of the term "alienation" appears to be an ambiguous comment on their situation. Political and social attitudes in modern
Britain are not clear-cut, and alienation is an ambiguous concept. What is clear is that the uncertainty about how young
people are integrated into the mainstream of adult society goes
to the central political questions in contemporary Britain: What
is the future of the mixed economy and the open society? Do
enough people care about it sufficiently to defend it? Can it be
made to work sufficiently well to hold off the Marxists on the
one hand and the exponents of the corporate state on the
other?

2

Young People and the Labor Market

It is necessary first to consider the fortunes of young people in the labor market against the background of demographic trends since the end of World War II, including changes in the birth rate, changes in the rate of staying on at school and college beyond the minimum school-leaving age, and changes in the proportion of the relevant age groups of both sexes available for employment.

Published information on the employment trends of young people is less than satisfactory owing in many cases to changes in the method of collection and in particular to the incompatibility of British labor statistics with those published by the United States and Japan and other OECD (Organization for Economic Co-operation and Development) countries.* Within these limitations, however, we can examine the British figures and determine how the trends of the 16-to-19 and 20-to-24 age groups compare with those of the rest of the adult community. We will discuss differences relating to wage differentials, employment protection, industrial relations, and the availability of

*Comparability between the U.K. and other members of the European Economic Community (EEC) will be remedied as results from the 1973 and 1975 EEC Labor Force Survey become available. The first impact of the survey can be found in "New Projections of Future Labour Force" (Department of Employment *Gazette*, June 1977, pp. 587–92).

social benefits. We will also consider some of the more vulnerable groups—those with the lowest educational qualifications, those belonging to ethnic minority groups, and those living in regions that have been particularly severely affected by rising unemployment during the present recession.

Demographic Background*

The pattern of the United Kingdom's birth statistics follows a familiar line. Immediately after World War II there was a baby boom. The birth rate subsided in the early 1950s but began to rise again in the mid-1950s and went on rising until 1964; since then there has been a continuous decline (Figure 2). The projected trend begins to rise again by the later 1970s, reaching another hypothetical boom by the year 1990. This upturn has been consistently forecast throughout the present decline on what may be called the "jam tomorrow" principle, but it has not so far shown overt signs of actually happening.

The downturn in the birth rate for the country as a whole cloaks important differences among social classes. Between 1970 and 1976 there was almost no change in the total number of births to families in professional, managerial, and administrative categories, while births to manual working-class families declined by about a third.

The population figures for the 15-to-19 and 20-to-24 age groups are now showing the consequences of the postwar fluctuations. In 1961, 15- to 19-year-olds numbered 3,695,000 and 20- to 24-year-olds numbered 3,306,000 (Table 1). By 1976 these figures had risen to 4,252,100 and 3,895,000, respectively. The 15- to 19-year-olds will peak in 1982 at 4,705,000. They represented 28.3 percent of the population available for employment in 1961; by 1971, those under 25 had increased to 31.5 percent of those economically active. However, the rise reflected an increase in the size of the total age group, whereas, except for married women, percentages of young people who

*Some of the figures used here relate to the U.K., some to Great Britain (excluding Northern Ireland), some to England and Wales only. This is because of vagaries in the system of statistical collection for different purposes. England and Wales account for 89 percent of the U.K. population.

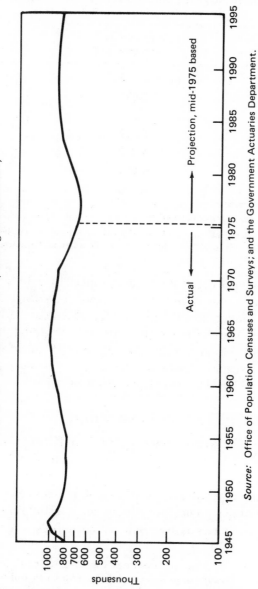

Figure 2. Annual births, United Kingdom, actual 1945 to 1975, and projected 1975 to 1995 (semilogarithmic scale)

Source: Office of Population Censuses and Surveys; and the Government Actuaries Department.

Table 1. Number of young persons aged 15 to 19 and 20 to 24,
United Kingdom, actual 1951 to 1971, and projected,
1976 to 1991 (numbers in thousands)

Year	15 to 19 years	20 to 24 years
1951	3,175	3,393
1961	3,695	3,306
1971[a]	3,832	4,237
1971[b]	3,860	4,255
1976	4,252	3,895
1981	4,691	4,276
1991	3,720	4,484

[a] Census estimates of resident population, *Annual Abstract of Statistics.*

[b] Estimates and projections based on mid-1974 estimates of resident population, *Population Projections 1974–2014,* Office of Population, Censuses, and Surveys.

were economically active declined, especially among those aged 15 to 19. A recent estimate of the labor force for 1977 showed that those under 25 available for employment had decreased between 1971 and 1977 from 5,102,000 to 4,964,000.* However, for this period, precise comparisons of labor-force participation rates cannot be made because of changes in the age breaks for which data are available (Table 2).

Educational Activity

Throughout the period since World War II, the proportion of those 15 to 19 remaining in full-time education has been increasing in Britain as elsewhere. Among those in their early twenties, the percentages are of course much smaller, but there has been a similar trend toward remaining in full-time education (Table 3). These trends are discussed more fully in Chapter 4.

*The labor-force estimate incorporates the EEC Labor Force Survey for 1975 as well as revisions of projections of the number of full-time students. The comparison of those under 25 who are economically active excludes students and only deals with those under 16, eliminating the problem of the removal of the 15-year-olds in 1974 from the labor force as a result of raising the minimum school leaving age to 16.

Table 2. Percentages of young persons in selected age
groups in the labor force, Great Britain,
1971 to 1977

Year	Men		Unmarried women		Married women[a]	
	15–19	20–24	15–19	20–24	15–19	20–24
1961	74.6%	91.9%	73.2%	89.4%	41.0%	41.3%
	15–17	18–24	15–17	18–24	15–17	18–24
1971	48.2	91.0	48.8	85.6	–	45.7
1972	52.0	91.7	48.8	84.0	–	45.7
	16–17	18–24	16–17	18–24	16–17	18–24
1973	62.7	90.6	57.0	83.5	–	49.7
1974	55.6	89.7	51.8	78.3	–	49.2
	16–19	20–24	16–19	20–24	16–19	20–24
1975	65.8	88.9	60.2	77.0	51.9	54.3
1976	64.7	88.5	58.8	76.7	51.9	54.6
1977	64.0	88.2	57.7	76.7	51.9	54.9

[a]There are no estimates of female students by marital status for years other than 1971, so the labor-force participation rates of married women for 1975 to 1977 include students. The number of married female students is small, and there is little difference between the rates including and excluding students.

Source: 1961–Decennial Census Data; 1971 to 1974–*General Household Survey*, Office of Population, Censuses and Surveys (London: Her Majesty's Stationery Office); 1975 to 1977 – "New Projections of Future Labour Force," *Department of Employment Gazette*, June 1977, pp. 587–592.

Table 3. Percentage of young people in full-time
education, by age, Great Britain

Age group	1961–62		1974–75	
15–19	21.0%		47.9%	
	Men	Women	Men	Women
20	6.6%	4.0%	13.3%	9.9%
21–24	3.6	1.1	6.3	3.8

First Employment

Information on first employment was collected until 1974 through the local education authorities' careers service. When a school leaver took a job, he or she had to get a national insurance card allocated through the careers office. The last survey made before these cards were disposed of (insurance numbers are now issued by the Department of Health and Social Security) shows that there were 512,648 school leavers aged 16 and 17 entering first employment. Among the big employers of male first entrants were manufacturing industries (36 percent), followed by construction and the distribution trades. Young women went in great numbers into public administration, utilities, professional services, and insurance and banking.

Table 4 shows the industrial distribution of first entrants in 1974 compared with the 1971 census, as well as with the two surveys carried out for the Manpower Services Commission in the winter of 1976. The MSC surveys concerned only 3,000 young people aged 16 to 19 and 550 unemployed young people.

Unemployment Rates: International Adjustments

British unemployment statistics differ in important respects from those assembled by the U.S. Bureau of Labor Statistics and, as a consequence, understate the rates of unemployment when compared with those calculated for countries that use the American method of collection.

An unemployed person in Britain becomes a unit in the statistics by registering for employment at a Job Center (or what used to be called a Labor Exchange). Only by registration can someone who is unemployed obtain unemployment benefits, but not everyone looking for a job (and not all those who register are looking for a job, though refusal to accept a suitable job should entail the forfeiture of benefits). If not every unemployed person registers, it follows that statistics based on registration are likely to understate unemployment. This is most obviously true in the case of married women (some of whom do not qualify for benefits if they have only paid half-rate insurance contributions), those who become voluntarily unemployed (and who are, therefore, not immediately eligible for benefit), and young people. Young people are not entitled to unemployment pay unless they have been working and making social insurance payments for a specified period, but they do qualify for means-tested supplementary benefits.

It is government policy to improve the employment services administered on behalf of the Department of Employment through the Employment Services Agency of the MSC. Behind the bureaucratic nomenclature lies the intention to make former Labor Exchanges more acceptable to users—hence the decision to rechristen them Job Centers—and take a leaf out of the private employment agencies book by making the Job Centers more customer oriented and attractive. Whether this has reduced, or will in time reduce, the amount of nonregistration, nobody can as yet say. The MSC only came into being under a law passed in 1974, and the first attempts to change its image have come against the background of already strongly rising unemployment figures.

To make British unemployment statistics comparable with those of other industrial countries under the terms of the International Labor Conference (1954) and the even more comprehensive definition of the U.S. Bureau of Labor Statistics, the unregistered category must, of course, be included. There are, however, two further categories that must be considered: those on temporary layoff and adult students seeking work. The United States definition includes both categories, the magnitude of which tends to be heavily dependent on the operation of the labor market in the country involved. There has been no tradition of students working during their education in Great Britain on the North American scale, but as the total number of students in full-time higher education has grown, so has the number of them who depend economically on working during vacations. Students are eligible for maintenance grants from the local authorities; in the case of students on degree courses these are mandatory, but many others are dependent on "discretionary" grants, which local authorities have been less willing to

Table 4. Distribution of workers of all ages and of young workers, by industrial groups, Great Britain, selected years, 1971 to 1976-77

Industrial Grouping	1971 census employment		Employees in employment, June 1974		1976 MSC 16-19 survey		1976-77 MSC un- employed survey
	All ages	15–19	All ages	First entrants	Employed	Unemployed	
Males:							
Extractive industries[a]	6.0%	5.8%	4.7%	5.6%	6.0%	1.0%	4.0%
Manufacturing industries	37.9	38.4	41.5	36.4	35.1	15.0	41.0
Construction	10.6	12.3	9.3	15.2	17.6	21.0	13.0
Utilities	2.0	1.5	2.2	1.1	1.5	b	1.0
Transport and communication	8.7	5.1	9.5	4.2	20.3[d]	31.0[d]	28.0[d]
Distribution	9.9	13.2	8.3	14.9			
Insurance, banking, and finance	3.1	2.3	3.9	2.6	4.0	b	0
Professional and scientific services	6.8	2.8	7.4	1.9	2.3	1.0	1.0
Public administration and defense[c]	7.4	7.0	7.3	7.2	5.2	6.0	5.0
Miscellaneous services	7.1	10.2	5.9	10.8	7.9	24.0	5.0

Females:

Extractive industries[a]	2.6%	0.8%	1.4%	0.8%	1.3%	4.0%	b
Manufacturing industries	25.2	35.0	32.1	31.1	32.4	28.0	43.0
Construction	1.1	1.1	1.2	1.4	1.6	4.0	1.0
Utilities	0.7	0.6	0.9	0.8	0.7	b	1.0
Transport and communication	3.0	3.0	3.7	3.1	} 25.1[d]	} b	} 34.0[d]
Distribution	18.0	21.6	14.1	25.8		36.0[d]	
Insurance, banking, and finance	5.5	10.0	7.4	11.8	10.7	4.0	2.0
Professional and scientific services	21.1	9.9	21.7	8.2	8.5	9.0	2.0
Public administration and defense[c]	5.4	4.6	7.6	5.0	7.8	4.0	2.0
Miscellaneous services	14.8	11.8	10.0	11.9	11.9	12.0	12.0

[a]Extractive industries include agriculture, forestry, fishing, mining and quarrying.

[b]Less than 0.1%.

[c]Defense not included in MSC surveys.

[d]Distribution and transport and communication not distinguishable.

Source: June 1974 data—Department of Employment *Gazette*, December 1975, p. 1272; and *British Labour Statistics Yearbook 1974* (London: Her Majesty's Stationery Office, 1976), p. 226. All other data—Manpower Services Commission, *Young People and Work* (May 1977), p. 13.

award in a period when public expenditure is being held down. Both mandatory and discretionary grants are subject to a means test of the student's parents unless the student is over 21 and has been self-supporting for three years. In recent years, the National Union of Students has discovered that the regulations governing unemployment benefits and supplementary benefits can be turned to the students advantage and has successfully organized the increased registration of students as unemployed during the vacations. In February 1976, it was decided to exclude adult students from the main unemployment statistics on the grounds that they had distorted the general picture for the previous six months.

The temporary layoff category depends on the decision when to collect information. In some surveys of the labor force, the relevant date is the day on which the information is collected. In the United States, only the individuals who are suspended from work for a complete week are counted. In Great Britain, workers are on temporary layoff usually for no more than two or three days in a week, but still on the employer's payroll, and it is regarded as misleading to include them in the unemployed total. Adjusting to the U.S. definition would, therefore, mean adding into the total labor-force figure those who are unregistered and unpaid family workers while deducting an estimated number who have crept into the statistics by doing more than one job. On the basis of the 1971 census, this would mean adding some 60,000 to make a grand total of 24.2 million in the labor force.*

The *General Household Survey,* in spite of its small size, produces the best published estimate of the unregistered and those on temporary layoff. Their estimate of the unemployed is much closer to that worked out by the Bureau of Labor Statistics than the figures published on a regular basis by the Department of Employment.

---

*Sources of information that are used to supplement the Department of Employment's figures (for example, for the unregistered) are the *General Household Survey* (annually from 1971), the EEC *Labor Force Survey* (biennially from 1975), and the census returns (which give snapshots of the employment situation in the census years—for our purposes, these are 1961, 1966, and 1971).

Table 5. Estimates of unemployment: Great Britain

Year	General Household Survey	Bureau of Labor Statistics (U.S. definition)	Department of Employment (excluding adult students)
1971	3.9	3.8	3.4
1972	4.2	4.2	3.7
1973	3.2	2.9	2.6
1974		2.9	2.6
1975		4.9	4.1

The unregistered unemployed, broken down by age group, using 1966 census data and the *General Household Survey* for 1972 and 1973, are shown in Table 6.

In general, the effect of the adjustments for unregistered people is to raise the published British unemployment rates, and the adjustment is especially large for the youth age groups. It is clear that unemployment generally has been on a rising trend: at each successive trade cycle, the level has risen more at the trough of the recession and gone down less at the top of the ensuing boom (Figure 3).

Against the background of the rising trend, the tendency has been for unemployment among young people under 25 to rise still more sharply, especially during the steeper recession of

Table 6. Estimates of the number of unregistered unemployed, Great Britain (numbers in thousands)

	1966		1972		1973	
	Males	Females	Males	Females	Males	Females
15–24	29.7	36.0	36.9	52.5	33.0	40.0
25–54	39.6	67.2	36.9	106.75	48.0	104.0
55–64	13.5	8.4	9.9	12.25	8.0	12.8
65 and over	7.2	8.4	6.3	3.5	11.0	3.2
Total	90.0	120.0	90.0	175.0	100.0	160.0

Source: 1966—census data; 1972 and 1973—*General Household Surveys.*

Figure 3. Number of unemployed persons, all ages and those under 25,
Great Britain, 1950–1976 (semilogarithmic scale)

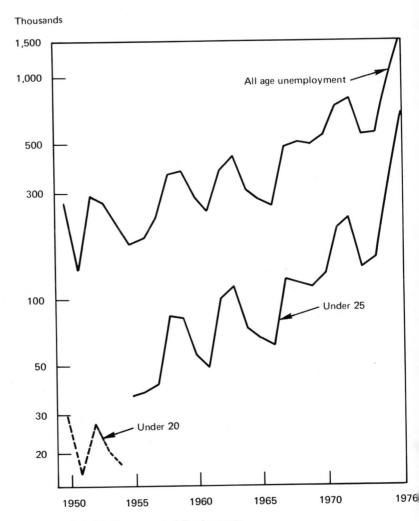

Source: 1950–64—Department of Employment;
1965–76—Parliamentary Question, November 17, 1976.

Note: Method of collection changed in 1955 to those unemployed under 25.

the mid-1970s. Table 7 shows the change in unemployment rates of young men and women between 1975 and 1977 in relation to those for the remaining age groups. Females were relatively better off in 1975, having an unemployment rate of 10.4 percent for those 16 and 17 contrasted to the male rate of 13.8 percent. This was no longer the case in January 1977, when the roles were reversed. But it can be seen that youth unemployment is running well ahead of the unemployment of other age groups.

Figure 4 shows the rising unemployment rate separately for men and women under 30 and for those 20 to 24. The rate among girls and young women has been higher than the overall unemployment rate throughout the period. But in the case of young men and boys, it was only in 1969 that their rising trend line crossed that for unemployment generally.

Table 7. Estimated unemployment rates by age, Great Britain, selected dates, July 1975 to January 1977

	Males				Females			
	July 1975	*January 1976*	*July 1976*	*January 1977*	*July 1975*	*January 1976*	*July 1976*	*January 1977*
7	13.8%	12.3%	26.7%	12.8%	10.4%	12.0%	25.6%	14.1%
9	9.6	11.2	10.7	11.1	6.1	8.1	9.2	9.9
4	6.8	10.0	9.3	10.1	3.1	5.3	5.9	7.0
9	5.2	7.0	6.6	7.3	2.1	3.1	3.5	4.4
9	4.4	5.9	5.6	6.3	1.0	1.5	1.8	2.2
9	3.7	4.8	4.6	5.1	0.9	1.2	1.4	1.7
9	3.7	4.7	4.6	5.1	1.3	1.7	1.9	2.2
d over	7.8	9.1	9.1	9.5	0.2	0.2	0.2	0.2
rall rate	5.4	6.9	7.2	7.2	2.1	2.9	4.0	3.8

*e: Department of Employment *Gazette*, July 1977, pp. 718–719.

Unemployment rates by age have not been calculated since the withdrawal of National Insur-
cards in 1974. The EEC labor-force data have been used with certain adjustments along with
nation from education departments for the younger age groups to give the estimates. Their
o runs: "While the figures are presented to one decimal place, they should not be regarded as
ing precision to that degree."

Figure 4. Unemployment rates of young persons relative to overall unemployment rate, by sex, Great Britain, 1966 to 1975

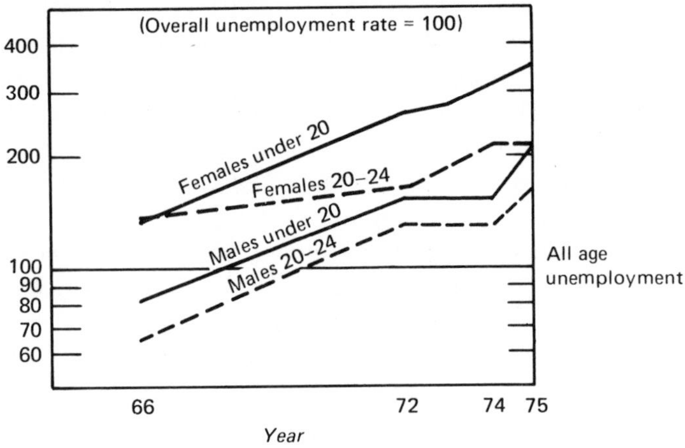

Source: Metcalfe, 1976.

Employment Forecasts

The forecasts set out in *Towards a Comprehensive Manpower Policy* (MSC, 1976) assume that between 1976 and 1981 the total labor supply could increase by 774,000, or about five times the increase between 1971 and 1976. This is made up of an increase in the male labor force of 220,000, an increase in the number of married women in the labor force of more than 500,000, and an increase in the number of young people entering employment of about 50,000. The MSC view (1977), which has not been challenged, is that "whether unemployment among young people is a structural or cyclical phenomenon, there will be relatively little improvement if total unemployment remains high or falls only slowly." It is assumed that a 3 percent rate of growth of output per annum is necessary to prevent the unemployment rate from continuing to rise, and that to return to full employment in five years would require an annual growth rate over that period of nearly 5 percent (National Institute for Social and Economic Research, 1977, p. 51). This is unlikely to be achieved in the present and prospective economic climate. The MSC (1977) concluded that past changes in occupational structure are unlikely to be reversed; that demand for unskilled and unqualified workers would continue to decline; and that the trend in conventional apprenticeships would be downward as the result of "de-skilling" more occupations, while demand for technicians and semiskilled workers would continue to rise somewhat.

Assuming that the key influence on youth unemployment is the level of total unemployment, the MSC (1977) offered three projections for the years between 1977 and 1980 (Figure 5). Each reflects the seasonal pattern of schooling, with the worst unemployment levels concentrated in the third quarter of the year. In the most pessimistic projection, youth unemployment rises to nearly 450,000 in 1978 and is still more than 350,000 in the third quarter of 1981. None of the projections sees youth unemployment peaking at less than 100,000.

Industrial and Trade-Union Policy

A recent MSC report (1976, p. 13) notes the especially rapid rise in unemployment among young people that occurred between July 1973 and July 1976: the proportion of total unemployment represented by those under 20 rose from 12.5 to 27.8 percent. The length of time young people were remaining out of work, though still on average considerably shorter than for older workers, has risen sharply. "Young people now account for a significantly larger proportion of longer term unemployment" (see Figure 6). The report recognized this as part of a longer-term tendency for youth unemployment to rise relative to the total and forecast that this "would continue, and might indeed be intensified because of the increase in the numbers of young people entering the labor force by 1981, and because employment protection legislation, etc., may make employers more reluctant to recruit additional employees" (MSC, 1976, p. 15).

As we saw earlier, the Labor Government of 1974 took office in a period of acute industrial strife. There were three parts to Labor's policy towards the unions. The first, which is not relevant to this discussion, involved a commitment toward

Figure 5. Unemployment among young people: projections of the
Manpower Services Commission, Great Britain,
quarterly, 1977 to 1981 (in thousands)

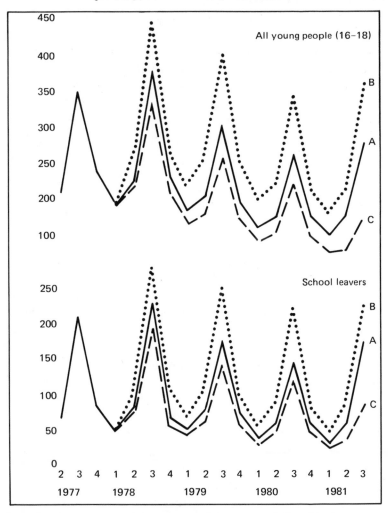

Projection A assumes a moderate recovery of the economy followed by two years
of improved employment before a cyclical decline in the early 1980s.

Projection B assumes that unemployment continues to rise before a similar
cyclical pattern of recovery occurs.

Projection C assumes that unemployment ceases to rise in 1977 and the recovery
of the economy is sufficiently sustained and rapid to approach full
employment in the early 1980s.

Source: MSC, 1976, p. 12.

Figure 6. Percentage distribution of medium-term and long-term unemployed, by age group, Great Britain, July 1974 to July 1976

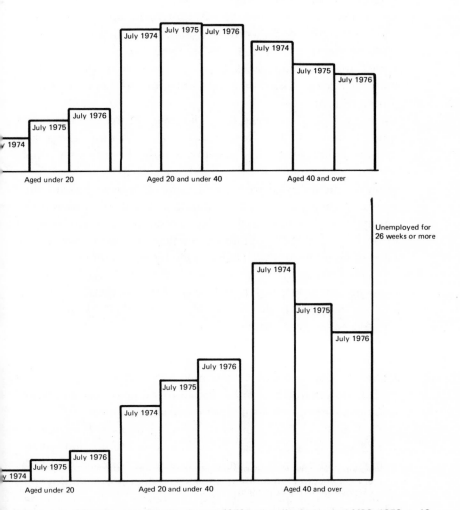

Source: Department of Employment *Gazette*, August 1976 and earlier issues; and MSC, 1976, p. 12.

worker participation in the direction of industry and the setting up of a commission to report on this topic. The second part concerned the repeal of labor legislation passed by the outgoing Conservative government, and in particular those parts of the 1971 Industrial Relations Act which curbed the power of the unions and limited their immunity at law. To do this, the Labor government brought in a Trade Union and Labor Relations Bill, which passed into law in 1974. This restored the unions' legal exemptions and gave them the power to enforce the closed shop. The third measure, the Employment Protection Act of 1975, strengthened collective bargaining as well as introducing a "bill of rights" for employees, ranging from guaranteed payments for those on short time to establishing the length of maternity leave with a guarantee of either the same or similar job on return.

The MSC's reference to employment protection legislation quoted above is, therefore, well taken: legislation has greatly increased the costs to the employer both of employing people and of laying them off. The law provides for a scale of minimum payments to all workers of more than two years standing who lose their jobs through redundancy, with the provision of an appeals procedure to independent tribunals in case of dispute. These legal minimum entitlements then become the basis of larger negotiated claims made by trade unions.

The effect of all this is to make job-protection legislation—not by itself, but together with the energetic defense of existing jobs by trade unions acting on behalf of threatened workers—a major consideration in the minds of management in contracting industries or in companies seeking to raise individual productivity by cutting staffing levels, who come to regard a declaration of "no compulsory redundancy" as their best, and perhaps their only chance of reducing the number of their employees without major industrial disruption.

Against the background of Britain's industrial decline, the rise of unemployment, and especially of youth unemployment, is not in itself surprising; indeed, any other outcome would be unexpected. There has been a steady reduction in employment in manufacturing, which in 1961 accounted for about 38 percent of all employment and in 1975 only 33 percent. The big growth areas for employment have been in local government and in service industries (Figure 7). Public-sector employees increased from 5.8 million in 1961 to 7.4 million in 1976. In terms of wages and salaries, this 27 percent increase in manpower pushed up the public sector's share in the national payroll to 30 percent compared with 24 percent in 1961.

Figure 7. Employment by sector, United Kingdom, 1959 to 1974

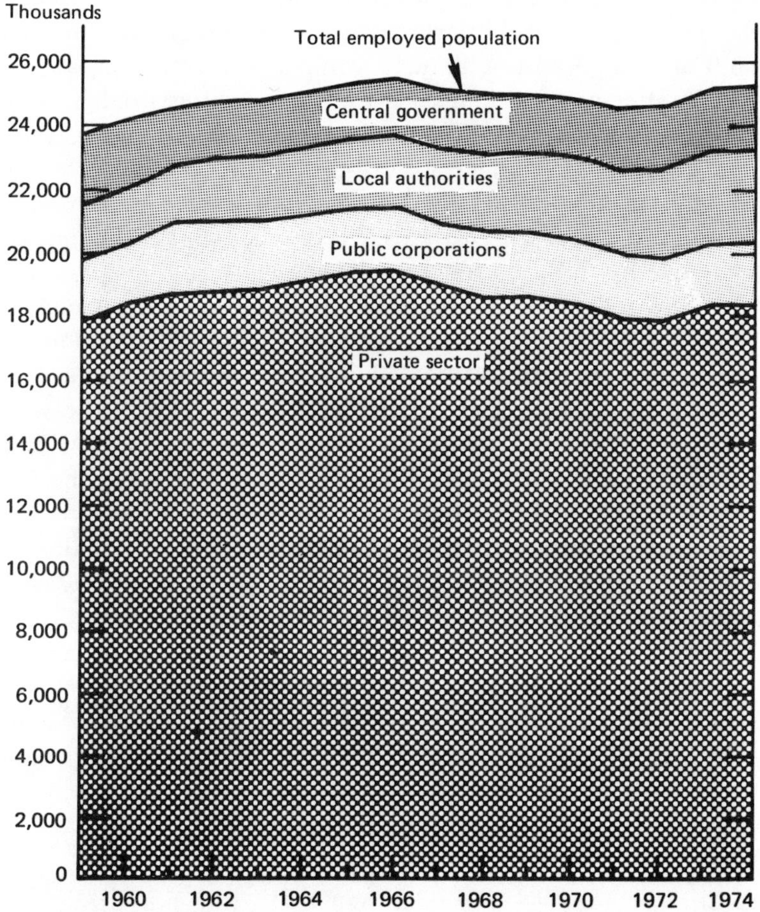

Source: Central Statistical Office

Wage Differentials

It has been suggested that one factor contributing to the increase in unemployment among the young—particularly school leavers and those under 20—is the reduction in wage differentials between adults and young workers. This can be seen from a comparison of earnings in 1968 and 1975. According to the *New Earnings Survey* matched sample,* in 1968 young men under 18 had median earnings amounting to 30.5 percent of all male workers' median earnings. By 1975 the percentage had risen to 42.5. A similar, though less marked, increase affected the 18- to 20-year-olds, whose median earnings were up from 55.9 to 65.6 percent of all male workers' median earnings.

In the case of female workers, the differential in 1968 was already less than for young men. Even so, among those under 18, the percentage rose from 53.6 to 63.5 while for 18- to 20-year-olds it rose slightly from 80 to 83.5 percent. The earnings of 20- to 24-year-olds, in contrast, remained about the same relative to the earnings of all women.

The reduction in the differential has been most marked since the government and the trade unions have joined in attempts to operate a wage policy that discriminates in favor of lower paid workers. The so-called social contract made between the government and the Trades Union Congress in July 1975 and July 1976 put specific limits on wage increases. The first contract restricted pay increases to £6 a week, a flat rate raise which automatically favored those at the lower end of the pay scale and did not allow for any increases for those earning more than £8,500 a year; the second contract was based on a formula which, in effect, also allowed lower-paid workers a bigger percentage raise than those with higher incomes.

Taken together with the tendency for collective agreements to specify the age of 18 for the introduction of adult rates (an increase from 38 to 67 percent of all agreements between 1970 and 1974), young people's pay raises have been

---

*The *New Earnings Survey* is an annual survey of employees by the Department of Employment from April 1970 (Great Britain) and from April 1971 (Northern Ireland). Results from September 1968 were based on a pilot study for the *New Earnings Survey*.

considerably higher in percentage terms than those of most employed people (Figure 8).

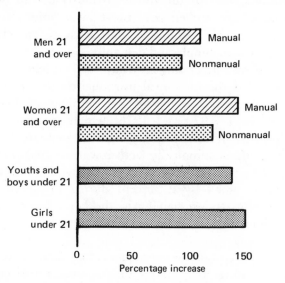

Figure 8. **Percentage increase in median gross weekly earnings of full-time manual and nonmanual employees,[a] by sex and age group, Great Britain, April 1970 to April 1975**

[a]Excluding those whose pay was affected by absence

Source: Department of Employment, *New Earnings Survey.*

The *New Earnings Survey* showed how this policy affected the earnings of young men and women between 1974 and 1975:

Table 8. **Percentage increase in average weekly earnings, by sex and age, Great Britain, 1974 to 1975**

	Men	*Women*
Under 18	73.3	59.0
18–20	50.3	49.0
21–24	35.4	41.7
All ages	29.5	38.7

Source: Department of Employment, *New Earnings Survey.*

It has to be conceded that pay increases on the order of those won by workers under 18 would be astonishingly high at any time. There is a bizarre coincidence between this movement in pay and a sharp recorded rise in youth unemployment, which might have been expected to reduce the bargaining power of young workers. Part of the rise is obviously due to the direct intervention of government and the trade unions through the social contract, which amounted in a sense to an attempt to suspend the laws of supply and demand.

To whatever effect this may have had on juvenile employment was added the piecemeal introduction of equal pay for women, another factor raising the earnings of lower paid workers. Between 1970 and 1976, female manual wages increased from 59 percent of the male equivalent to 71 percent. The number of economically active women rose 17 percent during the 20 years up to the 1971 census, while the active male labor force declined by 2 percent during this period. Thus, women entering and remaining in the labor force were competing in increasing numbers for marginal jobs with school leavers.

How to interpret the consequences of these sharp changes in relative earnings is a matter of on-going controversy. In a letter in *The Times* on November 15, 1976, Professor Wilfred Beckerman and seven other distinguished economists concluded: "There is now very substantial quantitative evidence that the 1966 increases in unemployment benefits, which halved the net cost of being unemployed, led to a substantial increase in the natural or equilibrium rate of unemployment. There has been an additional potent force at work for the last four years—the income policies of successive governments. These have had an effect broadly equivalent to introducing a minimum wage at 30 percent above the previous minimum. There is overwhelming evidence from other countries that the effect of a minimum wage law is to raise unemployment."

On October 6, 1966, the earnings-related supplement to the unemployment benefit was introduced. At that time the weekly supplement ranged from 5p (for annual earnings of £450 before unemployment) to £7 (earnings beyond £2,100).

The present supplement peaks at £12.18 for those earning in excess of £3,450. The earnings-related supplement can be claimed only after receiving unemployment benefits for two weeks and then runs for 26 weeks. The amounts available are shown in Table 9.

Table 9. Weekly unemployment and supplementary benefits, Great Britain, 1977

	Age		
	16	*17*	*18 & over*
Unemployment benefit			
Single person, plus earnings related element up to £12.18 for 6 months only	£12.90	£12.90	£12.90
Supplementary benefit			
Single (nonhouseholder)	£7.80 plus £1.20 rent	£7.80 plus £1.20 rent	£10.15 plus £1.20 rent
Married couple, both unemployed, any age (nonhouseholder)		£21.95	
with accommodation		£20.65 plus rent	

Source: Department of Health and Social Security.

Vulnerable Groups

Some young people are more vulnerable than others because they live in regions of the United Kingdom where unemployment is particularly severe. Table 10 shows how youth unemployment relates to adult unemployment in various parts of the country. It can be seen that the rise of youth unemployment has been relatively large in the hitherto prosperous southeast region since 1974. Although the increase during the recent recession has been least marked in Scotland and the north (with a historically high rate of unemployment), the actual levels of unemployment among young people remain highest in the traditionally less favored areas, as Figure 9 indicates.

Table 10. Unemployment by region, age, and sex, Great Britain, January 13, 1977

	Unemployed under 20		Unemployed of all ages		Percent change (under 20): from July 1974	
	Males	Females	Males	Females	Males	Females
Southeast	30,225	22,939	262,418	80,346	+314	+619
East Anglia	3,234	2,652	28,378	8,538	+347	+560
East Midlands	6,761	5,968	57,350	18,920	+162	+300
Yorkshire and Humberside	10,316	10,277	86,599	28,527	+120	+250
North	10,445	10,438	78,027	29,113	+ 63	+159
Northwest	21,615	17,425	151,762	51,201	+114	+270
West Midlands	12,344	12,087	94,441	34,689	+185	+396
Southwest	9,597	8,737	84,688	28,431	+288	+557
Scotland	22,509	18,458	129,306	54,112	+ 88	+240
Wales	8,352	7,949	61,042	22,330	+171	+289
Total	135,398	116,930	1,034,011	356,207	+152	+318

Source: Department of Employment Gazette, February 1977, biannual tables on age and duration of the unemployed by region, pp. 136–137.

Figure 9. Unemployment rates of persons under 20 years of age, by region, Great Britain, January 13, 1977

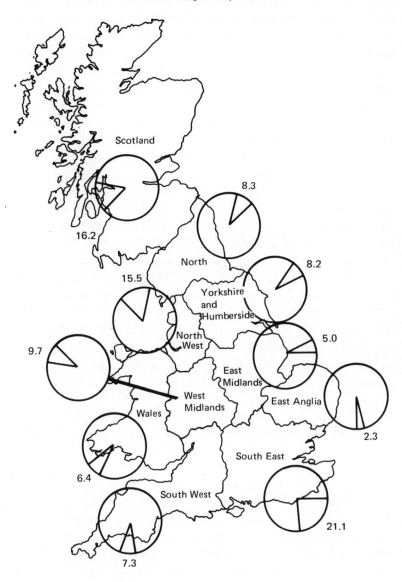

Young people are more likely to change their jobs during the first years of employment and are most likely to be offered temporary jobs than men and women in older age groups. This is partly a reflection of restlessness and experimentation on the part of the young themselves, and it is partly inherent in the kinds of jobs young people, especially those with modest qualifications, are likely to be offered. Between 1972 and 1974, there was some evidence from the *General Household Survey* that job changing was on the increase. Whereas in 1972 about a quarter of the relevant age groups changed jobs, by 1974 this had gone up to nearly one third.

School leavers with poor educational qualifications are certainly among those most vulnerable to unemployment. A survey carried out in 1972 by the National Youth Employment Council brought this out very clearly. Only about 11 percent of the young people registered at Careers Offices had passed any recognized school examinations. That means that 89 percent were drawn from among the bottom third of the academic range who left school with no diploma. Since 1972 this tendency has continued: the least well qualified suffer most. The proportion of those who have passed at least one examination has risen to 80 percent, but so too has the chorus of complaints from employers about the poor educational standards of potential recruits. Attention, therefore, has been focused on the academic achievement of young school leavers, and there have been attempts to link this with their employment prospects—a belief that "If only they had better qualifications in the basic subjects they would be able to get work." There is no evidence that this is so. An inadequate level of public education might contribute indirectly to the structural weakness of British industry or even to the political inadequacy of economic management at the national level. But there is no reason to suppose that were there suddenly to be an increase in the proportion of pupils passing examinations, this would lead to substantially more of them being employed until eventually the present recession is succeeded by more buoyant economic circumstances. A trend toward achieving more basic knowledge might, however, lead more boys and girls to stay on in full-time education, thereby removing some potential job seekers from the statistics.

The most obvious of the vulnerable subgroups is that composed of members of ethnic minorities, mainly West Indians and Asians. The ethnic minorities have worse employment prospects than the rest of the population at all stages of the cycle: even when there is full employment, although they benefit with the rest of the community, they are always likely to have difficulty in obtaining employment commensurate to their education and talents.

The 1971 census showed that those of "new Commonwealth" origin constituted 2.2 percent of the economically active population. Estimating minority group unemployment levels is complicated by the large number who fail to register and are therefore likely to be left out of the official statistics. The Community Relations Commission (1976) estimates that up to 50 percent of young West Indians are unregistered, and statistics in general reflect only recent immigrants—the definition of ethnic minorities extends only to first- and second-generation immigrants from certain countries of the Commonwealth and Pakistan—and the numbers consequently are very small. The following data show the increase in unemployment of the minority men and women under the age of 25 since 1974:

	February 1974	February 1975	February 1976	February 1977
Males	2,676	5,231	11,966	12,301
Females	832	1,906	5,280	7,012
Total	3,410	7,137	17,246	19,313

Unemployment among the registered minority group workers under 25 increased more than fourfold between 1974 and 1977, during which period it only doubled for the rest of the population.

According to the 1971 census, unemployment among West Indian youth was already twice the national average:

	All males	West Indians	Indians	Pakistanis
Great Britain	8.1	16.2	6.7	6.8
South East	7.0	15.8	6.8	5.2

Once again regional imbalance is accentuated. Nearly half of all ethnic minority unemployment is to be found in the Southeast, in particular in London. A recent study of London (Lomas, 1975) referred to the "high level of unemployment among young black people" which "gives rise to particular concern. Minority unemployment is chiefly a problem of the West Indian community and is concentrated largely among the under 25s. The numbers are rising. In some parts of London, one in four of the total unemployed is colored. The average period of unemployment for this group is lengthening."

In the case of young Asians, difficulties caused by prejudice and discrimination are compounded by differences in culture, religion, and family background. They are often academically successful and well adjusted at school and often leave their native lands with unrealistic expectations. A recent survey (Community Relations Commission, 1976) found that more than half of those questioned in a sample of over a thousand minority people expected to go on to further education in medicine, law, or some other profession. High expectations are easily frustrated, however: 60 percent of those questioned found it difficult to get the jobs they wanted. In many cases they blamed this on racial discrimination. According to another study by the Community Relations Commission, now known as the Commission for Racial Equality (December 1976), this understates the full measure of the local problem. In one London borough, Lewisham, young West Indians made up 40 percent of those registered as unemployed. In the case of Asian minorities, up to 50 percent are likely to remain in education in pursuit of high qualifications after completing compulsory school. But even if they are disappointed in the jobs which eventually materialize, their prospects are in general much better than those of the West Indians and more likely to take them into higher status occupations.

3

Youth Employment and Industrial Training

Industrial education and training have been the subject of prolonged debate since the end of World War II, culminating in 1973 with the Employment and Training Act, which created the Manpower Services Commission (MSC) to preside over manpower, employment, and training services, including many of the functions formerly undertaken by the Ministry of Labor (renamed the Department of Employment).

The history of industrial training in Britain is complex. The 1944 Education Act (like the 1918 Education Act before it) envisaged the development of part-time day-continuation schools (part-time schools for apprentices or persons in other types of training), modeled loosely on the lines of the German *Berufschule*. After World War I, attempts to go ahead were impeded by the postwar slump, and after World War II, the "county colleges"—the 1944 version of the day-continuation schools—were given low priority compared with the reform of the secondary system and the provision of extra places and teachers for the enlarged school population. By the end of the 1950s, the raising of the school-leaving age from 15 to 16 (completed in 1972–73) had displaced day-continuation schools as the favored next stage of educational reform, and the voluntary extension of day release tailed off.

All of these proposals for day release (one or two days off per week to attend classes) for young workers assumed that industrial training was the responsibility of industry. The colleges of further education—providing a variety of vocational, technical, and general courses at many different levels for students of 16 and older—worked closely with industry to provide educational services where necessary. Traditionally, these services had been offered in night school and evening classes, but part-time and full-time day courses were coming to the fore. Vocational education was not seen as the job of the secondary schools in the postwar era (except in a few areas such as shorthand and typewriting). Both industry and educators regarded vocational education as industry's affair.

Apprenticeship remained the main instrument of industrial training, usually carrying with it admission not only to the traditional craft lore but also to the craft trade unions. Craft apprenticeship was largely a male realm. In all, some 24 percent of entrants into employment were admitted to apprenticeship in 1974; 43 percent of all boy entrants and only 6 percent of girls (mainly in hairdressing). Tables 11 and 12 provide a breakdown of the type of employment of new entrants.

For many reasons the tradition of apprenticeship has been a liability. The mechanisms of apprenticeship have always been restrictive, designed to bind the apprentice to his master and to restrict the master in the admission of others to his field of mastery. This mechanism has placed industrial training squarely within the arena of industrial relations and made the quality of training secondary to the maintenance of industrial peace and the exploitation of the temporary strengths and weaknesses of industrial management and trade unions. The maximum age of admission to apprenticeship is also important in the circumstances of a developing education system. It relates to the duration of the training period, which in turn relates to the level of pay for apprentices, the age at which they become eligible for the full adult rate, the time it takes to train a specific level of skill and the issue of whether all apprentices need the same training period. All these matters become further complicated because of the need to facilitate adult retraining and because

	Apprenticeships	Employment leading to qualifications	Clerical	With training	Other
Males:	100.0%	100.0%	100.0%	100.0%	100.0%
Agriculture, forestry, fishing, mining, and quarrying	3.7	1.5	0.9	4.9	9.2
Manufacturing	39.3	18.5	19.2	41.0	35.1
Construction	24.4	8.2	3.4	7.6	9.6
Transport and communications	3.9	4.3	10.7	4.4	2.9
Distributive trades	4.8	4.8	8.1	18.1	29.0
Administration, professional services, etc.	10.1	57.0	54.1	14.1	5.1
Hotels, personal services, etc.	13.8	5.7	3.6	9.9	9.1
TOTAL, all industries and services (100.0%)	43.0%	1.3%	7.0%	17.1%	31.6%
Females:	100.0%	100.0%	100.0%	100.0%	100.0%
Agriculture, forestry, fishing, mining, and quarrying	0.8	0.1	0.4	0.6	1.3
Manufacturing	6.4	4.7	23.4	54.4	34.4
Construction	0.5	0.5	3.2	0.3	0.2
Transport and communications	0.4	0.4	5.4	4.0	0.6
Distributive trades	5.2	2.5	13.4	20.1	48.7
Administration, professional services, etc.	11.7	87.8	49.0	14.3	3.9
Hotels, personal services, etc.	75.0	4.0	5.4	6.3	10.9
TOTAL, all industries and services (100.0%)	6.5%	1.8%	40.5%	17.2%	34.0%

Source: *British Labor Statistics Yearbook*, 1976, p. 226, Table 100.

Table 12. Numbers of young persons entering employment, by age and class of employment, Great Britain, 1965 to 1974 (numbers in thousands)

| | Age at entry into employment | | | | | | | |
| | Boys | | | | Girls | | | |
	15	16	17	Total	15	16	17	Total
1965	201.2	66.9	23.2	291.2	188.4	56.6	23.6	268.5
1966	185.7	64.2	20.3	270.2	176.1	53.8	21.8	251.7
1967	167.2	66.4	19.3	252.8	159.1	53.9	21.0	234.0
1968	164.7	70.2	20.9	255.8	154.9	55.8	21.8	232.4
1969	158.8	74.4	20.9	254.1	149.4	57.5	22.0	228.9
1970	148.9	76.9	22.3	248.2	141.9	58.1	23.8	223.8
1971	146.0	74.8	21.4	242.1	141.4	56.5	22.5	220.4
1972	151.2	82.9	24.8	258.9	143.6	59.9	24.8	228.2
1973	15.0	96.9	28.6	140.5	10.5	69.4	27.2	107.0
1974	—	254.8	20.0	274.8	—	217.0	20.9	237.8

	Apprenticeship to skilled occupation	Employment leading to recognized professional qualifications	Clerical employment	Employment with planned training apart from induction training, not covered in previous columns	Other employment	Total
Boys						
1965	118.1	4.4	29.1	37.0	102.6	291.2
1966	114.4	3.5	24.7	35.3	92.3	270.2
1967	107.7	3.3	22.1	32.9	86.8	252.8
1968	110.0	3.1	21.3	34.2	87.1	255.8
1969	108.2	3.1	21.2	35.5	86.0	254.1
1970	104.9	3.3	19.8	35.2	85.0	248.2
1971	95.6	3.1	17.6	38.7	87.1	242.1
1972	100.2	3.4	18.4	42.6	94.3	258.9
1973	66.0	3.3	17.8	20.4	33.1	140.5
1974	118.2	3.5	19.2	47.0	86.9	274.8
Girls						
1965	16.6	4.6	108.2	33.7	105.5	268.5
1966	16.7	4.4	101.0	34.4	95.2	251.7
1967	16.8	4.3	91.7	32.5	88.7	234.0
1968	17.1	4.3	90.3	33.6	87.1	232.4
1969	16.3	4.1	90.8	34.7	83.0	228.9
1970	15.8	4.1	89.5	34.0	80.4	223.8
1971	16.7	4.1	78.8	37.5	83.4	220.4
1972	18.0	3.9	78.3	40.5	87.5	228.2
1973	5.0	4.0	62.3	12.4	23.3	107.0
1974	15.5	4.2	96.3	41.0	80.9	237.3

Source: British Labor Statistics Yearbook 1974, page 223, Table 96.

the development of industrial technology does not conform to the lines of demarcation rigorously laid down between craft unions.

Thus, the reform apprenticeship has been on the agenda since the end of World War II, and at each turn in the development of public policy on industrial training, attempts have been made to loosen the rigidity of the system and to increase its adaptability to modern conditions.

In 1964, the Industrial Training Act brought into being industrial training boards for each industry, charged with the overseeing of training policy. This act also brought in the principle of levy and grant: companies within a given industry had to pay a levy on their staff roll. This was paid into a fund from which grants were made to companies according to the training they engaged in, provided they conformed to the training policies laid down by the Industrial Training Board. The effect was to stimulate training activities and the growth of training staffs and, especially in the case of engineering and the construction industries, to encourage the reappraisal of skill-training schemes and their reorganization on a modular basis in conjunction with colleges of further education. More and more of the first year of training has been conducted off the job in college or group-training centers.

In 1973, the levy-grant system was modified. The rate of the levy was limited to a maximum of 1 percent of payroll and there was provision for a wide range of exemptions. The work of the industrial training boards was augmented by the formation of the Training Services Agency (TSA), with substantial funds (£110 million in 1976) to support and promote industrial training. The MSC and TSA have an existence outside government but are financed from public funds and staffed by civil servants. Thus they have more independence of action than a government department while still being essentially part of the public service. Six of the ten Manpower Services Commissioners are drawn in equal numbers from industrial management and the trade unions, with minority representation of local government and education. This alliance between the Confederation of British Industries and the Trades Union Congress gives the MSC its muscle and at the same time limits what can and cannot be done. During its short life so far, the commission has been strongly backed by the government with funds and political support, and, because the Labor Party is currently dominant, the trade-union leadership in the MSC has been particularly strong.

Statistical Background

Statistics about the training and allied vocational education of young workers are far from perfect. The method of collection is such that the classifications used may not be interpreted in a uniform manner. As a starting point for policy making and action, however, the Training Services Agency has used analyses based on the census returns and figures collected by the National Youth Employment Council (1974).

Between 1964 and 1974, the total number of young workers under 18 declined by one-sixth (MSC, 1975). There were several reasons for this: smaller age groups, the raising of the minimum school-leaving age, more voluntary staying on beyond 16, and higher youth unemployment. More than half the boys, but only one in eight of the girls, were in apprenticeships or other employment with planned training extending beyond 12 months (Table 13). Another small group of boys and girls were receiving training of from two to twelve months. In the case of girls, a large group (40 percent) were in clerical occupations where the amount and quality of training for many is virtually nonexistent, especially in various office operations that have been divided into their component parts so as to require minimal instruction. In the case of both boys and girls, about a third of those entering employment, in addition to those listed above under the clerical work heading, receive training of less than eight weeks.

When the apprenticeship figures were analyzed, they showed marked regional differences reflecting the industrial structure of the country. Pupils stay on at school longer in the Southeast (where proportionately fewer enter apprenticeship) and have more opportunity for professional training and clerical

Table 13. Distribution of boys and girls entering employment by class of employment entered, Great Britain, 1964 to 1974

Employment entered[a]	1964		1970		1972		1974
	000s	*%*	*000s*	*%*	*000s*	*%*	*000s*
Boys							
Apprenticeship	114.5	36	104.9	43	100.2	40	118.2
Professional	5.2	1	3.3	1	3.4	1	3.5
Clerical	34.0	11	19.8	8	18.4	7	19.2
Employment with planned training over 12 months	30.5	10	20.7	8	23.8	9	26.4
Employment with planned training 8 weeks– 12 months	16.5	5	14.6	6	18.8	7	20.5
Other employment	114.2	37	85.0	34	94.3	36	86.9
Total	314.8	100	248.2	100	258.9	100	274.8
Girls							
Apprenticeship	16.9	6	15.8	7	18.0	8	15.5
Professional	5.0	2	4.1	2	3.9	2	4.2
Clerical	114.9	39	89.5	40	78.3	34	96.3
Employment with planned training over 12 months	13.3	5	11.0	5	12.6	6	13.5
Employment with planned training 8 weeks– 12 months	24.4	8	23.0	10	28.0	12	27.5
Other employment	119.0	40	80.4	36	87.5	38	80.9
Total	293.5	100	223.8	100	228.2	100	237.8

[a]The classification embraces training of all types—off the job, on the job, and simple experie training—and includes provision for further education in some instances.

[b]Provisional (analyses by age, region and industry not yet available). The figures for the year probably affected by the raising of the school-leaving age in 1973.

Source: Manpower Services Commission, 1975, page 4, Table 2.

employment than in the less prosperous North, where there is more employment in heavy industry as well as more craft apprenticeship (Table 14).

A major concern over the past quarter of a century has been the extent to which access to industrial training has fluctuated with the state of the economy. Persistent shortages of skilled labor have been found at all phases of the economic

Table 14. Percentage of boys obtaining apprenticeships, by region, Great Britain, 1962 to 1972

Department of Employment Region	1962	1964	1966	1968	1970	1972
London and Southeast	27	26	30	32	32	28
East and South	34	36	41	42	41	36
Southwest	38	38	40	39	37	34
Midlands	35	35	42	44	43	37
Yorkshire and Humberside	44	45	51	51	51	47
Northwest	44	43	51	49	48	46
North	41	41	50	48	47	47
Wales	26	29	37	38	36	33
Scotland	39	40	45	46	47	45
Total Great Britain	36	36	42	43	42	39

Source: Manpower Services Commission, 1975, p. 5, Table 3.

cycle, accentuated by the employers' practice of reducing their intake of trainees when the economy is in recession (Figure 10). The result of their actions is not fully felt until the economy has begun to operate at a level nearer to full capacity, when the apprentices who would then have been completing their training are missed. When confidence returns, the recruitment of apprentices increases, and by the time they are trained, the cycle has entered another phase.

Many of these problems are highlighted in the training experience of the engineering industry. In recent years, the British engineering industry has reflected the poor performance of Britain in world markets. Between 1967 and 1974, engineering employment (as a percentage of all employment) declined from 19.5 to 15.5 percent. In the 10 years to 1974, the number of

Figure 10. Cyclical variations in apprentice intake and total notified
vacancies (all industries and services),
Great Britain, 1962 to 1972

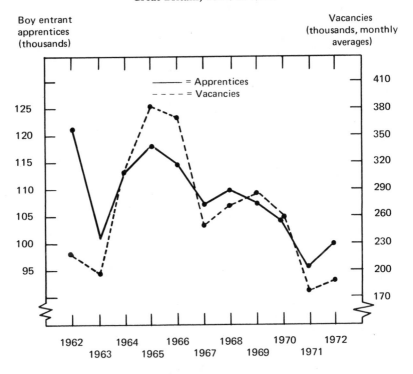

Boy entrant
apprentices
(thousands)

Vacancies
(thousands, monthly
averages)

Source: Manpower Services Commission, 1975, p. 6.

engineering apprentices dropped by about 40 percent, while the
total number of skilled workers employed in engineering
dropped from 830,000 to 688,000 (a 17 percent drop).

Attempts have been made to increase the annual intake of
engineering apprentices, which fell from about 20,000 in the
late 1960s, to 12,000 in 1972–73, and by 1974 was back to
18,700. The intake of technicians has followed the same trend.
A recent report stated that "it now seems inevitable that there
will be in 1976–77 and the two subsequent years fewer craftsmen available than employers will wish to employ" (Engineering
Industries Training Board, 1975, p. 23). In fact, even in a period

of high unemployment there is a recognizable shortage of skilled labor.

Engineering apprenticeship, however, even in a period of juvenile unemployment, is not oversubscribed. Fewer "well qualified" young people are now said to be seeking engineering training. Some possible reasons for this have been put forward in a paper by Gerry Eastwood (1976), trade union leader, and general secretary of the Association of Pattern Makers and Allied Craftsmen for the British North American Committee. This paper points to the rapid erosion of the differential between skilled and unskilled wages. Using figures collected by the Department of Employment for men's wages in the engineering, shipbuilding, and chemical industries, Eastwood calculates that the differential advantage of skilled time workers (paid by the hour) over nonskilled time workers dropped from 44 percent to 32 percent. According to his reckoning, a 16-year-old apprentice in 1976 could expect to receive £17.85 a week (or 42.5 percent of the full craft rate), while a 16-year-old junior manual worker without training or obligation to study could earn £17.

Analysis and Proposals

Long-term training. It is generally agreed that there have been considerable improvements in the quality of long-term training, including apprenticeship, since the early 1960s, although a great deal more remains to be done. (See Chapter 4 for a discussion of short-term measures to increase both training and employment.) The Industrial Training Boards have gone a long way toward systematizing training programs and requiring an effective combination of on-the-job training with off-the-job vocational education. More flexibility has been introduced, and there are more courses aimed at providing a common preparation for more than one craft skill. Less rigid rules about the age of entry into apprenticeship have been negotiated, but this has usually meant no more than extending the range of possible exceptions to otherwise restrictive regulations; the use of these exceptions still depends on the liberalness of employers and local union branches. Considerable progress has been made on adult retraining, with official union support but not without reserve at grass-roots level. This same reserve extends to most attempts to admit young adults to apprenticeship.

In the summer of 1976, the MSC and the Department of Employment put forward a scheme aimed at insulating long-term training more effectively from short-term economic considerations. The proposals recognized that many essential skills were not peculiar to individual companies but extended across companies on an industry-wide scale. Firms that trained too few of their own apprentices relied on recruiting those trained by others. Persistent "poachers" thus saved money on the cost of training by living off the public-spirited activities of others, while restrictive trade-union practices inhibited the normal market mechanisms that might otherwise have compensated for fluctuations in the trade cycle.

The core of the MSC/Department of Labor proposals was a scheme of collective funding to cover the first, most expensive part of the apprentice's training course, mainly off the job in a further-education college or group training center. Without specifying details, the proposal assumed that more than half the cost would be borne by an expanded levy on payrolls and the remainder by a government grant. Collective funding was justified on the grounds that a shortage of skilled manpower was damaging to the national economy. It was, therefore, linked to the idea of a manpower analysis that would identify national needs for particular kinds of skill.

In the months following publication of the proposals, *Training for Vital Skills* (MSC, 1976), the trade unions welcomed the recommendations, while opposition from employers mounted. The trade unions welcomed the idea not only because they recognized a shortage of skilled workers but also because they wished to see the proportion of young people in recognized forms of training increase and because their collectivist inclinations led them automatically to favor the injection of public funds. The initial readiness of the employers' organizations to cooperate cooled as grass-roots hostility to the scheme emerged during consultations. What happened, in fact, offers an instructive commentary on the politics of industrial training within the larger field of British industrial relations. During the months following the publication of *Training for Vital Skills,* the parliamentary position of the Labor government weakened. Some by-election results, including the loss of two Labor seats, encouraged the Conservatives and strengthened the resolve of employers who believed that under a Conservative government the present strength of trade-union representation on the MSC would weaken. Because of the erratic course of public policy in this area of industrial affairs over the past 15 years, there is no confidence that any controversial policy can actually be carried through, and this gives the maximum incentive to resolute opposition and determined temporizing on the part of those waiting for another swing of the political pendulum.

With regard to the proposal for collective funding and a systematic attempt to increase training for specific skills, the employers have one powerful argument on their side. While accepting that there is a general shortage of skilled labor, they accuse the unions of creating artificial shortages by maintaining narrow and unrealistic job classifications that prevent the efficient distribution of the skilled workers now available. Nobody doubts that there is a great deal of truth in this accusation, which links up with the larger criticisms of overmanning and low productivity in British industry. The employers see the proposal for collective funding and the expansion of apprenticeship as an attempt to dodge the issue and further strengthen the restrictive practices that were established to defend freehold rights in traditional skills.

This is another example of industrial training issues being subsumed within the larger debate on industrial relations—a debate in which rational argument is much less important than economic power. The response of the MSC (where the trade unions are the dominant voice) is to step back now to prepare for a jump forward later and to remit the whole question to further study (and further delay) by a committee of labor and management representatives.

The episode shows the narrow angle of vision adopted in Britain in consideration of public policy for those under 18. The formal theory maintained is that industrial training is a purely technical affair of concern largely, if not exclusively, to employers and trade unions. The argument is reduced to questions of specific shortages of skill and specific restrictive practices by trade unions, about the precise numbers of workers who should be admitted to particular crafts, how their training should be paid for, how long it should last, and who should be allowed to enter a haven that could easily become overcrowded.

The policy makers are aware that there are other considerations. They compare Britain, where only 30 percent of employed youth under 18 are in some form of long-term planned training, with West Germany, where the equivalent figure is more like 70 percent. They recognize that a well-organized period of training for an older teenager in industry is a worthwhile and formative experience, even if it does not lead to life-time employment in the particular industrial context in which the training was received. They believe that no special disadvantages would attend training more than might appear to be needed to fulfill specific manpower targets; that, in any case, versatility is the principal requirement; and that versatility is more likely to be cultivated by sound initial training than by none. But the policy makers are imprisoned within an administrative structure that limits the range of arguments that can be brought into play. The larger social considerations are in the realm of educational policy, while manpower and industrial training are more down to earth. The language of industrial training policy has to reflect this: objectives must be defined in economic terms, and a managerial structure must be designed to achieve them. Thus the policies affecting the 40 percent who remain in full-time education and those affecting the 60 percent who enter employment are sharply divided; the departments of employment and education, who are responsible for the young people concerned, remain at arm's length, divided not only by function but also by philosophy; and an overarching policy for the youth under 18 years old in the community as a whole remains an elusive and apparently unattainable ideal.

Short-term training. As has been noted, the majority of young people entering employment, if they receive any instruction, receive only modest forms of industrial training or on-the-job training lasting less than a year. In many cases, the kinds of jobs young people enter require only limited training. A few industries receive large numbers of youths into these low-skill jobs. One in six boys and one in four girls entered the distributive trades in 1974. Boys are heavily concentrated in engineering (17 percent), miscellaneous services (11 percent), and construction (15 percent). Girls go in large numbers into the manufacture of clothing and footwear (7 percent) and textiles (16 percent).

The MSC (1975, p. 11) cites examples of short-term training from the clothing, hosiery, and knitted-goods sectors. "In clothing, training currently takes about eight weeks. This often takes the form of supervision of developing machine skills, rather than training in manipulative skills; training specific to the particular task in mass production could take only four weeks. In the hosiery and knitted-goods sector, training up to experienced worker standard takes 12 to 16 weeks." The policy of the industrial training boards is to encourage the further systematization of short-term training, and there is evidence that this has been happening in recent years. But there are limits to what can be done within the present assumptions.

Relatively few of those receiving short-term training get day release to colleges of further education. Some of the larger organizations, especially among the nationalized industries and public services, offer day release for general education (Table 15)—the old county-college idea surviving in attenuated form, but only on a small scale.

Employers in general are more prepared to consent to day release—often it is strongly encouraged by industrial training boards—when it is directly linked to vocational education, and in the great majority of cases this means for apprentices only (Table 16). Nonvocational day-release classes are notoriously difficult to teach and, of course, this is especially true when the students are boys and girls in jobs requiring the least vocational instruction, who tend to have been the least successful and the least well motivated at school.

Currently, however, the most obvious need for improvement is not in vocational training but in general education, with

Table 15. Young people under 18 on day-release work, England and Wales, November 1971 to November 1974

Industry:	Men					Women				
	1971[a] as percentage of number insured	1971	1972	1973	1974	1971[a] as percentage of number insured	1971	1972	1973	1974
Agriculture, forestry, and fishing	39%	6,017	6,474	5,281	5,482	9%	311	343	298	364
Mining and quarrying	53	5,249	3,867	2,992	3,587	24	124	116	105	131
Manufacturing industries	42	82,136	69,916	63,427	69,572	7	12,153	9,957	9,215	10,302
Construction	48	22,874	27,810	31,180	27,149	8	424	449	404	397
Gas, electricity, and water	96	5,178	4,606	3,750	3,862	35	932	796	773	983
Transport and communication	46	8,650	7,704	6,630	7,065	18	1,840	1,846	1,328	1,592
Distributive trades	6	5,414	5,446	4,425	4,373	2	3,387	3,398	2,527	2,570

Insurance, banking, finance, and business services	9	754	693	970	1,319	2	692	619	727	1,220
Professional and scientific services	37	4,270	4,411	4,638	4,330	26	7,990	7,407	6,662	6,366
Miscellaneous services	36	20,191	21,129	19,626	17,275	24	12,646	13,785	10,586	10,073
Public administration and defense	107	10,289	10,778	10,030	10,418	74	7,511	7,258	6,108	7,781
Total	36	171,022	162,834	152,949	154,432	10	48,010	45,974	38,733	41,779

aNumbers on day release at November 1971 as a percentage of those insured at June 1971. No equivalent figures available for later years.

Source: Department of Education and Science, *Statistics of Education*, 1974, Vol. 3.

Table 16. Comparison in selected industries of boys under 18 receiving
further education and percentage of new entrants taking apprentice
training, Great Britain, 1971

Industry	Percentage receiving further education	Percentage taking apprentice training
Food, drink, and tobacco	15	12
Mechanical engineering	75	69
Vehicles	59	71
Textiles	9	13
Gas, electricity, and water	93	76
Administration and defense	100	41

Source: Manpower Services Commission, 1975, p. 13, Table 4.

some outspoken criticism of the academic achievements of
those entering employment. This criticism has been articulated
by the Training Service Agency and has helped to fuel wider
demands for more accountability from the school system and
closer supervision of school curricula by the Department of
Education and Science. Thus, at the lowest level of skill as well
as at the highest, the distinction between vocational and general
education breaks down. The raising of the school-leaving age
from 15 to 16 might have been expected to help, but better
basic standards of competence cannot be expected in the short
term. It is, of course, doubtful whether the benefits of extended
compulsory education will take a form satisfactory to employers, who are as concerned about attitudes and values among
alienated young people as they are about levels of mathematical
or reading ability. This is especially true in inner-city areas,
where poor employment prospects and a dispiriting social environment combine to produce negative attitudes both to education and to work long before the end of the secondary school
course.

One response, in Britain as elsewhere, has been to draw
attention to the importance of career counseling. In the English
context, a clear distinction has to be made between career

teaching (teaching about careers and the world of work, under-taken by the regular staff of secondary schools) and career guid-ance (counseling and advice provided by vocational guidance staff from outside the school). A career guidance service is organized by each local education authority for the schools under its control (see Chapter 5) and is staffed by specialists whose counseling duties also include the provision of a place-ment service for school leavers' first employment. The quality varies according to the adviser's knowledge both of education and of industry. The guidance that 14- and 15-year-olds require is as likely to be educational as industrial, and the adviser needs to be well informed about the basic qualifications needed for entering all forms of qualified work, about the local availability of vocational courses in colleges of further education, and about the choices involved in continuing education at school. The MSC—possibly because it undervalues the importance of the link between vocational and educational guidance at this level and suspects that local career advisers are inadequately in-formed on the needs and opportunities of industrial employment—believes that responsibility for career guidance should be taken away from the education authorities and trans-ferred to the MSC itself, which is responsible for employment services for the adult population. The education authorities (and the teachers and educational administrators) believe equally strongly that career guidance should continue to be a part of the education service.

The local career service, though separately administered by each local education authority, provides a career structure that is national rather than local. A career adviser is likely to work for a number of different local authorities in the course of his or her career. While the quality of the service inevitably varies to some extent from one authority to another, the existence of this national career structure helps to counter some of the more obvious parochial limitations of a local service.

In recent years more emphasis has been placed on educa-tional guidance in English schools (and still more in Scottish schools). Further, because of the development of larger schools (as a result of the creation of comprehensive secondary schools in place of separate grammar and secondary schools), there has been a greater willingness to allow guidance and counseling to emerge as teaching specialties. However, this development has depended mainly on the policy of individual schools and head teachers rather than on any national initiative or decision by local education authorities. There is a long-standing tradition in English education that the general counseling function (as opposed to counseling specifically related to careers) is part of the professional responsibility of all teachers, and educators are reluctant to allow it to be concentrated in the hands of a team of specialists, as it is in North America. But however attractive the tradition may be in theory, it has often failed to produce either good career teaching or counseling. The unevenness of the services provided among various schools and education authorities has attracted much criticism. A survey undertaken by Her Majesty's Inspectors of Schools for the Department of Education and Science in 1971–72 (Department of Education and Science, 1973) found that career counseling within the schools is seriously inadequate. While 94 percent of secondary schools in England and Wales had at least one member of staff designated as careers teacher, in nearly half the schools the time set aside for this work only amounted to 20 percent of one teacher's time. One school in four provided no careers education for pupils 14 years and older.

There have been many suggestions that one way of improving career teaching would be to attack the isolation of the teaching profession and to encourage more teachers to learn about industry at first hand. One method would be to require, or at any rate encourage, would-be teachers to spend a minimum period in employment before entering teacher training. Another would be to expand small-scale schemes like the one now run by the Confederation of British Industries for practicing teachers who are given leaves from their schools for periods of industrial experience. It has so far proved extremely difficult to get beyond the talking stage, however, because of the considerable cost involved in even a small expansion of such schemes, and perhaps also because most public statements on this subject seem to express conventional pieties rather than real conviction.

For the 300,000 or so boys and girls who start work each year and receive no long-term training, the TSA proposes the development of "gateway" courses "of a recognized national standard . . . to enable young people to undergo vocational preparation off the job. The courses would inculcate knowledge relevant to jobs within broad occupational bands, and their length should depend on the time required for the young people to absorb the content—say, in many cases, three months" (MSC, 1975, p. 20). These courses would be conceived of as continuing basic education, vocational education, and industrial training, and would not only be simply a variant of those already provided by further education colleges: they would include an element of induction training.

A similar idea arose in the Department of Education and Science, and this has come to fruition in a scheme known as "Unified Vocational Preparation," which was launched in November 1976 on an experimental basis. As first announced, the projects were for "16- to 19-year-olds who leave school and go into jobs with little or no further education or training" and "will provide a basis for planning future provision for this age group" (Department of Education and Science, 1976b). Some were to be located in colleges of further education, others in TSA skill centers and on employers' premises. While it is too soon yet to assess the lessons learned from the pilot schemes or to draw conclusions from them about the feasibility of a national scheme, it appears to have been very difficult to get the pilot projects off the ground. The pilot scheme was only intended to involve 6,000 young people throughout Great Britain, and it looks as if even this modest goal will take several years to achieve. It has proved much more difficult to get employers to grant young workers the three-month block release to attend the courses than had been expected, notwithstanding the government wage subsidies of £10 per worker. In some cases, quotas have been filled by recruiting youngsters who have not previously secured employment or by incorporating unified vocational preparation into work-experience schemes. (See Chapter 4 for a description of the work-experience scheme.) It already looks unlikely that block release will be used in future to the exclusion of other forms of part-time and day release.

It is disappointing that the experiment was on such a limited basis and that the preliminary difficulties proved so formidable. To make a success of these courses, some hitherto unsolved educational puzzles have to be tackled; hopefully some important lessons can be learned from the various approaches being tried out in the pilot projects. Many of those who take part will be resistant to learning because of their school experience. In many cases, the courses will represent an attempt in three months to repair the results of educational failure over many years. The TSA recognizes also that a majority of employers are skeptical about the need for, or value of, more initial training for the group of young workers who now receive least. Furthermore many courses will take place in colleges of further education along with other courses for 16- and 17-year-olds who are expected to be maintained by their parents or who at most are eligible for exiguous maintenance allowances. Assuming that more than half the boys and girls entering employment from school each year need these courses, it is worth asking whether they should not be provided within the framework of secondary education instead of outside it.

4

Changes in Education and the Consequences

The development of the English educational system has passed through several phases in the years since World War II.* The basic education law passed in 1944 remains in force and still provides the framework within which development takes place. The relationship between the central government's Department of Education and Science (DES) and the local education authorities that administer the public system remains largely unchanged except for one major legislative innovation (in 1976) which laid down a national policy of comprehensive secondary schools and gave the DES power to insist on the provision of nonselective schools.

Changes in Primary and Secondary Education

The pre-1944 education system provided for nine years of compulsory education. Children entered the public elementary schools at five; at eleven those successful in a scholarship examination, plus those who could satisfy a minimum entrance standard *and* whose parents chose to pay the necessary fees, transferred to publicly maintained and grant-aided grammar

*Material concerning primary and secondary schools refer to England and Wales; Scotland has its own education laws. Most information in the section on universities (pp. 73-83), however, is collected on a "Great Britain" basis.

schools. Of all elementary school leavers, about 13.5 percent made the transfer to grammar school. The remainder stayed in the elementary schools. In some areas 13-year-olds in elementary schools have the chance to transfer to technical schools. Two-thirds of them left at age 14, and of those who stayed beyond their fourteenth birthdays, all but a handful had entered employment by the time they were 15, with or without further training.

Of those who went on to grammar school, nearly half left at age 16 after the first external examination—the School Certificate. Those continuing on to the sixth form included students taking the Higher Certificate examinations, from which the entrants to the universities were drawn. The winnowing process was severe: in 1938 there were 908,000 18-year-olds; of these, only 1.7 percent went on to university and 2.7 percent went on to all forms of higher education. Of the 15,500 university entrants, only 4,225 were from "grant-aided" schools. ("Grant aided" in this context covers all schools maintained by local authorities or otherwise receiving grants directly from public funds.) A private school system flourished alongside the system of schools paid for, or assisted by, public funds. The private school sector was very small compared with the grant-aided sector but provided a high proportion of those who completed the full secondary course and went on to the universities.

The pre-1944 education system was divided, therefore, into an elementary system from ages 5 to 14; an overlapping secondary system running from ages 11 to 16 or 18; and a parallel system of private or independent schools (which included the English "public" schools).

The 1944 Education Act made important changes. The minimum school-leaving age was raised to 15 in 1947, and provision was made for it to be raised to 16 in 1973. Instead of elementary schools and secondary schools overlapping each other, all children (except those in private schools) were to start in primary schools at age 5 and transfer at age 11 to secondary schools. All fees were abolished in the secondary schools and, decade by decade, the numbers of students in the secondary schools staying on beyond the minimum leaving age have risen.

Meanwhile, there has been some contraction in the private sector, but 6 percent of all pupils remain in the private primary ("preparatory") and independent secondary schools (which include the "public" boarding schools) although costs and fees have soared.*

Figure 11 shows how the profile of the education has developed since 1961-62. The funnel remains narrow but the base has widened, and there has been some widening all the way up as the rate of attrition has been slowly reduced. But the ambiguities in the concept of secondary education for all have inhibited this process of change to a mass system.

In general terms, the structural changes initiated by the 1944 act can be seen as transition from a narrow, exclusive system to one with much more open access. But the transition is far from complete. The secondary school curriculum is geared to an elite academic program, early specialization in academic subjects, advanced work on a narrow front in the last two or three years at school, and a pattern of specialized first degrees in the universities. The universities themselves have been geared to selecting students on a competitive basis. They have combined this selective entry with a short (three-year) first degree and a low dropout rate (14 perccent)—all of which has reinforced the dichotomy between "academic" and the "non-academic" students within the schools.

This dichotomy has dominated the development of the post-1944 secondary school. At first there was a large measure of agreement that if secondary education was to be provided for everybody, it had to be provided in separate forms: an academic form, corresponding to that of the traditional grammar schools (once the only form of secondary education), and a "modern" form for the less academically oriented pupil. There was also the suggestion that between the grammar schools and the modern schools, there should be "technical schools," but few of

---

*Combining some characteristics of both the maintained and independent sectors were the "direct grant" schools, supported partly by fees and partly by direct government grants, where at least 25 percent of the places had to be free. The direct-grant system is not being phased out as part of the government's plans for comprehensive secondary schools.

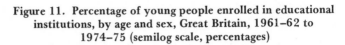

Figure 11. Percentage of young people enrolled in educational
institutions, by age and sex, Great Britain, 1961–62 to
1974–75 (semilog scale, percentages)

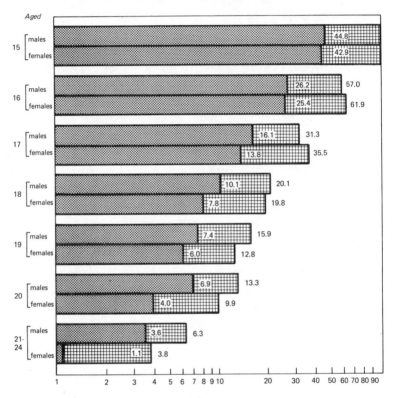

1961–62: *Source:* Committee on Higher Education, 1963.
1974–75: *Source:* Department of Education and Science, 1974.

these were provided, and many local authorities never built
them into their secondary systems.

The grammar schools took roughly the top 25 percent of
IQs; the modern schools took the rest. Each local authority ran
its own "11-plus examination" to decide which children should
go to which schools. During the 1950s, the change from the
prewar system was considered a triumph for liberal reform. By
abolishing fees, an attempt had been made to free educational

opportunity from its historic connection with parental wealth. The secondary selection procedures purported to examine the potential of each child and discover latent talent which could be allowed to flourish within the meritocratic ideals of the time. In this there was, of course, a great deal of wishful thinking; no diagnostic testing devices existed that could fulfill this specification, but the wish behind the thought was essentially that of the liberal reformer.

Within limits, the new secondary schools were remarkably successful. They certainly did expand opportunity, though the social-class composition of the grammar schools was still heavily skewed toward the middle classes. In addition, the selection tests used were not culture free and the limited experiment in equality of opportunity resulted in a continuing inequality of outcome. But the numbers completing secondary education rose steadily after 1950, as did the numbers staying on beyond the minimum school-leaving age and those taking the main examinations at 16—the General Certificate of Education at ordinary level (GCE-0 level) and the new Certificate of Secondary Education (CSE) which was initiated in 1965. Increasing numbers of students also qualified at the advanced level of the General Certificate of Education (GCE-A), as reflected in the growth of numbers in higher education at the universities and in the polytechnics, colleges of education, and other colleges of further education where higher education courses were developed.

The rapid growth of higher education in the 1960s is the most obvious fruit of the first postwar reform of secondary education, which expanded the maintained grammar schools and created a structure of selective and nonselective schools based on the 11-plus examination. But just when this expansion was at its height, the liberal conscience of the social democrats in the Labor Party turned against the grammar school, the meritocratic ideal, and the 11-plus selection process as negations of all that universal secondary education stood for. There had always been left-wing critics of the selective system. Some large local education authorities, including the one in London, had long committed themselves to the idea of comprehensive schools. (As early as 1934, London's Labor politicians had demanded "multi-type" or "multi-bias" schools, where all children of secondary age could be schooled together.) By the time the Labor Government of 1964 was formed, comprehensive schools had become an article of party faith.

The years since 1964 (but for the 3-1/2 years when the Conservatives were in power and Mrs. Margaret Thatcher was Secretary of State for Education and Science) have seen steady progress toward comprehensive education. In 1966 about a quarter of all secondary school children were in comprehensive schools. By 1976 the proportion had risen to three-quarters. The Education Act of 1976 was intended to set the seal on the transition. The Conservatives resolutely opposed the bill, believing that it should be left to the local education authorities to decide what kind of secondary organization they preferred. If there is a change of government at the next election, the Conservatives are pledged to repeal the act, but the movement toward comprehensive education may already have gone too far for them to halt it.

The transition to comprehensive education has undoubtedly led to some disruption and disturbance, and it will be some years before the necessary administrative adjustments have been made at the sixth-form level to insure that teaching resources are used in an economic manner. There is some evidence that the change to comprehensive organization has been accompanied by a deterioration of examination performance. It looks as if the combined effect of comprehensive reorganization and the raising of the minimum school-leaving age to 16 was to interrupt, if only temporarily, the trend toward more voluntary staying on to age 17. But it remains a matter for debate whether comprehensive reorganization, as such, will produce its own boom in further and higher education, comparable with the boom that followed the expansion of the grammar schools in the 1950s. Experience in Scandinavia and elsewhere has suggested that it should do so, provided the structure of postsecondary education is sufficiently flexible to accommodate new forms of student demand.

To date, the reform of English secondary education has not been accompanied by any national attempt to explore the curricular consequences of institutional change. The organizational changes have been carried through on the assumption that comprehensive schools simply provided a fairer, more effective way of offering the same curricular programs as had hitherto been offered in the various separate schools. Now, however, as the last phase of comprehensive secondary reform unfolds, educational debate has suddenly taken a sharp conservative turn. Both political parties have responded to public anxiety about educational standards by emphasizing the importance of public accountability. The Department of Education and Science has entered the debate about curriculum and examinations, criticizing progressive methods and demanding more carefully defined objectives for a core of studies for all students. The emphasis in the political discussion of education has changed with startling rapidity since the prime minister initiated a process of review in a major speech in October 1976. For 20 years past, the dominant educational concerns of left-wing English politics have been social equality and compensation for social disadvantage, the role of educational policy within the wider framework of social policy, and the expansion of opportunity for social mobility. Now the focus is on the links between education and the world of work, on the contribution the schools make to the preparation of men and women for work in the wealth-generating sectors of the economy, and thus on the transmission of essential skills for productive life.

This change of direction will not encourage the kind of curriculum and examination reform to which the secondary reorganization policy might otherwise lead. A long, drawn-out review of the secondary school examination structure is in hand. This is directed at broadening the 16-plus examination by combining the GCE-0 and CSE examinations within a single system of exams and at broadening the sixth-form course to a nucleus of five subjects instead of the present three. But there is obvious anxiety lest more changes lead to a decline in levels of attainment just when public concern about educational standards has become a matter of political debate. And behind this anxiety lurks the larger doubt about whether the educational needs of the economy are best met by putting more and more students through a watered-down academic program.

The more likely next step is a partial reorganization of educational arrangements for the 16 to 19 age groups. Support has been growing for a new range of "tertiary" institutions combining the several forms of full- and part-time courses, academic and vocational, for people 16 years and over. Upper secondary schoolwork, preparing some people for higher education, demands highly qualified staff who could be used more effectively if larger teaching groups could be established in tertiary institutions. Many sixth forms in comprehensive schools are now very small, and, because of the declining birth rate, are destined to get smaller. There is already some overlap between the secondary school sixth forms and the existing colleges of further education. Thus there are several administrative advantages to tertiary institutions, which could also provide a more adult atmosphere for older teenagers.

However, the same academic tradition that is undergoing anxiety about educational standards will resist any attempt to dismantle the traditional sixth form, which is regarded as the jewel in the secondary school crown and the guarantor of high standards of teaching in lower grades. This tradition also stresses the value of continuity and a smooth transition from stage to stage and reflects a strong conviction that time will be wasted and momentum lost if a major institutional change is scheduled at age 16. (There are also solid institutional obstacles in the way of a change across the board, relating to teachers' salaries and career structure.)

Whatever happens, the time may be coming when the present boundaries between secondary and postsecondary education have to be redrawn. In recent years the number of students under the age of 18 in the colleges of further education has grown steadily. There are now (1975) some 130,000 full-time and 526,000 part-time students under 18 enrolled in colleges. Some 80,000 students (mainly 19 and under) were enrolled in full-time further-education courses leading to the main, recognized school qualifications—GCE-0 and GCE-A, Certificate of Secondary Education, and the Scottish Certificate of Education. Another 239,000 were working for similar exams in part-time day or evening courses.

Higher education is defined in the British context as post-secondary education beyond the advanced level of the General Certificate of Education or similar standard. The universities, colleges of education, and colleges of further education where advanced work is undertaken (notably the polytechnics) provide the institutional resources of higher education. The growth of numbers in these institutions can be seen from Table 17.

It is likely that in the 1980s, the argument about institutional hierarchies and social discrimination in higher education will become more intense. The existence of a high-prestige "autonomous" university sector and a separate, much more varied, low-prestige public sector (the polytechnics and advanced further education) is in itself seen by many as a divisive barrier to the attainment of a greater equality in education. The differences in prestige of the two sectors are reflected in differences of administration. The autonomous sector is financed through a University Grants Committee, deliberately designed as a buffer between the government as paymaster and the universities as "chartered" bodies. The public sector, in contrast, is both financed and controlled by government, central and local, and such institutional freedom as has been attained by these colleges is much more circumscribed than that of the humblest university. It will have to be an object of policy to develop an administrative structure that can accommodate considerable diversity without institutionalizing this in a form seen as unacceptably divisive.

Changing Patterns of Postsecondary Education

The development of the nonuniversity sector of higher education was a major feature of the decade from 1963 to 1972. It was based on the expansion of both the colleges of education and the colleges of further education and the designation some of the latter as "polytechnics," offering an alternative to the universities for degree students. It was intended that these institutions should be more responsive to the needs of government, industry, and commerce than the universities and should aim to provide courses with a more professional orientation. But the

Table 17. Number of students enrolled in postsecondary education, by type of institution,
United Kingdom, 1964–65 to 1974–75
Home and overseas students
(numbers in thousands)

| | Universities[a] | | | | | | Colleges of education[b] | Advanced courses in establishments of further education[c] | | | All students |
| | Full-time | | | Part-time | | | | | | | |
	Under-graduate level	Post-graduate level	Total	Under-graduate level	Post-graduate level	Total	Full-time	Full-time (including sandwich)	Part-time day	Evening only	
1964–65											
Men	83.0	20.5	103.5	8.8	6.9	15.6	21.7	47.1	58.0	51.0	296.9
Women	34.0	5.4	39.5	1.7	1.4	3.0	51.9	10.3	2.8	2.0	109.5
Total	117.0	26.0	143.0	10.5	8.2	18.7	73.6	57.4	60.8	53.0	406.5
1966–67											
Men	112.4	25.8	138.1	2.9	11.3	14.2	27.9	47.2	62.1	48.5	338.0
Women	44.4	6.7	51.1	1.4	1.8	3.3	70.3	13.3	4.0	3.7	145.7
Total	156.8	32.4	189.3	4.4	13.1	17.5	98.2	60.5	66.1	52.2	483.8
1968–69											
Men	127.1	30.0	157.1	3.0	14.3	17.4	32.5	63.3	70.3	42.1	382.7
Women	51.9	8.4	60.3	2.0	2.5	4.5	86.0	20.2	5.6	4.4	181.0
Total	178.9	38.4	217.4	5.0	16.8	21.8	118.6	83.5	75.9	46.5	563.7
1970–71											

Men	133.9	33.1	167.0	3.0	14.9	17.8	34.4	72.7	69.8	39.8	401.5
Women	58.6	9.7	68.3	2.3	3.2	5.6	89.4	24.8	6.7	5.0	199.8
Total	192.4	42.8	235.3	5.3	18.1	23.4	123.8	97.5	76.5	44.8	601.3
1972–73											
Men	134.7	35.8	170.5	2.1	16.2	18.2	37.5	78.1	68.5	34.5	407.3
Women	65.2	11.1	76.3	1.4	4.0	5.3	89.7	29.9	8.7	4.9	214.8
Total	199.9	46.9	246.8	3.4	20.1	23.6	127.2	107.9	77.2	39.4	622.1
1974–75											
Men	136.3	36.1	172.4	1.8	17.1	19.0	32.5	84.1	76.5	33.7	418.1
Women	72.8	12.5	85.3	1.6	4.9	6.4	85.0	37.4	12.9	5.4	232.5
Total	209.1	48.6	257.7	3.4	22.0	25.4	117.5	121.5	89.4	39.2	650.6

aFrom 1971–72 on, students at universities on courses "not of a university standard" are included in the figures for undergraduate level.

bPublic sector and assisted only.

cExcluding departments of education in polytechnics, but prior to 1973–74 Northern Ireland students on teacher training courses at the Ulster College are included.

Source: Department of Education and Science, Education Statistics for the United Kingdom (London: Her Majesty's Stationery Office, 1976), p. 61, Table 39.

distinction between the sectors in terms of philosophy and function has not been easy to maintain; nor has it yet been as important as the distinction between different forms of financing and administration.

British policy has assumed that the number of teacher-training places should be related to manpower planning forecasts of the likely number of teachers required. This now means sharp and swift reductions in teacher-training numbers and a rapid, painful, and highly disruptive reorganization in which many colleges are to be closed or merged. Many will cease offering teachers' courses and become part of the larger pattern of further and higher education by developing other kinds of degree or diploma courses.

The prospect of any substantial development of two-year postsecondary courses in the near future does not look bright. The attempt to promote the two-year diploma of higher education through the Council of National Academic Awards (CNAA—the national body set up to supervise nonuniversity degrees) has so far met with only modest success. The diploma of higher education and the diplomas of the Technical Education Council and the Business Education Council could provide a structure of two-year qualifications on which to build, and this could be seen as a logical progression from development through the 1960s and the early 1970s, but the momentum has been lost and must be re-created.

The assumption in the government's 1972 white paper, *Education: A Framework for Expansion* (Department of Education and Science, 1972), was that the public and private sectors should continue to grow, but that the main expansion should be in the public sector, reaching parity in size between the two sectors by the early 1980s. This posited a 1981–82 higher education population of 750,000. Since 1972, projections have been scaled down several times—in the 1975 Public Expenditure White Paper to 600,000 and in a government statement early in 1977 to 560,000. The main reason for the reduction in planned growth (and therefore lower levels of planned public spending) is a reduction in the forecast level of demand in the early 1980s. The projections of the growth of the number of school students attaining the minimum level required for university entry were lowered in the light of figures collected for 1974 and 1975. The strong trend toward more advanced-level candidates that characterized the 1960s has been faltering. Since 1975, demand has shown some signs of hardening, but the prospects of a demographic downturn in the 18-to-24 age group by the late 1980s leads the government to believe that pressure of numbers will only be temporary and that long-term expansion should be governed by the long-term trend. (The most recent figures take account of the expected effect of higher fees on the recruitment of overseas students.)

The number of 18-year-olds in the age group peaks in 1982 at 924,000 (about 100,000 more than in 1977) and then begins to decline. No official forecasts of university enrollment extend beyond 1981. The Association of University Teachers (AUT) has published its own study (1977), which concludes that there will be a reservoir of women and older students to accommodate a continuing rise in university places even after the size of the relevant age groups begins to decline. Table 18 shows the AUT projections. Government assumptions about the supply of qualified candidates are much less sanguine, and there is a greater inclination to consider contraction of higher education as a possible way of reducing demand on exchequer resources, which could be diverted to other social purposes.

The AUT suggestion that adults will enter higher education in much larger numbers reflects a continuation of present trends and a belief that government policy and trade-union policy will promote these trends. Some growth in the number of older students seems virtually certain, though the immediate effect of cutting down the number of teacher-training places has been greatly to reduce opportunities for older students (especially women). But there are, as yet, no British equivalents at the conventional university level of the open-access arrangements found in North America; nor is there a policy such as that in Sweden, whereby a specific amount of working experience is accepted in lieu of academic entry qualifications. Individual universities, notably Sussex, have small-scale schemes. Most university regulations provide for the waiving of entry requirements in

Table 18. University student enrollment projections,
United Kingdom, 1974–75 to 1987–88

Source of projected changes	1974–75	1981–82	1985–86	1987–88
1. Male undergraduates of U.K. origin under 25 (very slow growth comparable with recent years)	115,000	119,000	121,000	122,000
2. Female undergraduates of U.K. origin under 25 (growth at the same rate as past 10 years)	64,000	93,000	115,000	116,000
3. Change in numbers due to population from 1974–75 level (assuming constant Age Participation Rate [7% in 1974–75], and effective length of undergraduate course, i.e., 3 years)	– – –	26,000	25,000	19,000
4. Undergraduates (male and female) of U.K. origin over 25 (continuing growth rate since 1968–69)	12,000	19,000	25,000	28,000
Subtotal of undergraduates (1 + 2 + 3 + 4) of U.K. origin	191,000	257,000	286,000	285,000
5. Undergraduates from overseas (male and female) (from 1977–78 stabilized at numbers in 1976–77)	12,000	15,500	15,500	15,500

6. Postgraduates from overseas (male and female) (from 1977–78 stabilized at numbers in 1976–77)	16,000	17,500	17,500	17,500
Subtotal of overseas students (5 + 6)	28,000	33,000	33,000	33,000
7. Postgraduates (male and female) of U.K. origin (assuming postgraduates of U.K. origin are a constant 15.62% of undergraduates of U.K. origin-position in 1976–77)	32,000	40,000	45,000	45,000
Subtotal of postgraduates (6 + 7)	48,000	57,500	62,500	62,500
Subtotal of undergraduates (1 + 2 + 3 + 4 + 5)	203,000	272,500	301,500	300,500
TOTAL UNIVERSITY ENROLLMENT (1 + 2 + 3 + 4 + 5 + 6 + 7)	251,000	330,000	364,000	363,000

Source: Association of University Teachers, *University Student Numbers*, April 1977, p. 7, Table 8.

Note: In the context of the vested interests of British university teachers, public policy toward overseas students has a major bearing on the totals; but the conclusions about home students generally are highly relevant to the British youth scene.

exceptional cases, but few exceptions are made. Similar exception clauses are usually provided by polytechnics and further-education colleges offering CNAA degrees, and in some cases these have been very liberally interpreted. However, at the national level there has been little governmental encouragement of policies supporting adult education. "Recurrent education" and "continuing education" have not captured the imagination of U.K. politicians as they have in Scandinavia or in France. The Trades Union Congress has spoken up for wider opportunities for older students but has not shown much conviction on the subject, except insofar as specifically trade-union adult education is concerned.

The Open University (OU), however, has in seven years done more than any other British institution of higher education to demonstrate the possibility of running high-quality courses for adults, many of whom lack the formal qualifications that the universities would demand. Present enrollment in the OU is about 56,000, and so far 21,230 students have graduated. Much attention has been focused on the social composition of the OU student body and on the high proportion of teachers among the initial intake (see Table 19). The OU acknowledges that the students who enroll for courses are likely to include more middle-class occupations than in the community as a whole but points out that if note is taken of their father's occupation instead of their own, they have a much more working-class complexion. The OU provides a further ladder of opportunity, in fact, for those working-class-born men and women who have already become socially mobile before they enroll in OU courses—a means for those who have already made it to make it a bit better.

Earlier official assumptions that the nonuniversity sector would get the lion's share of growth are increasingly challenged. It now seems more reasonable that the universities should have first claim on available students, and there is a tendency to give more respect to traditional public preference (as expressed by student choice) along with more conservative attitudes toward education policy generally. This disposition is powerfully reinforced by convincing evidence amassed by the universities that

Table 19. Occupation of provisionally registered students in 1971 by faculty, Open University, Great Britain

	Total students	Arts	Social science	Math	Science
Base: all students = 100%	*24,220*	*7,751*	*7,970*	*6,901*	*6,790*
Occupation	%	%	%	%	%
Housewives	9.3	15.7	12.5	4.1	4.9
Armed forces	1.7	0.8	0.9	2.5	2.3
Administrators and managers	5.2	4.7	6.0	5.7	5.1
Education	37.0	41.1	45.1	31.4	27.2
Professions and arts	8.9	11.9	11.7	5.3	7.3
Scientists and engineers	6.5	1.6	1.5	12.1	11.9
Technical personnel	12.4	2.7	2.9	21.4	24.2
Skilled trades	1.7	0.6	0.9	2.2	2.6
Other manual	1.4	1.4	1.2	1.1	1.6
Communication and transport	0.8	0.9	0.7	0.9	0.9
Clerical and office workers	6.7	9.6	7.7	5.3	4.0
Shop and personal services	3.3	3.7	3.7	2.3	3.3
Retired, not working	1.6	2.2	1.7	1.3	1.1
No information	3.3	2.9	3.3	4.2	3.2

Source: McIntosh, Calder, and Swift, 1976, p. 90, Table 10.

Note: The McIntosh, Calder, and Swift study was of the first cohort entering the university. In this cohort, some white-collar groups, notably nongraduate teachers, were more strongly represented than in subsequent years. Only 17 percent of OU students are from routine nonmanual and manual occupations. Reclassified according to their fathers' occupations, however, the percentage rises to 65 percent (see McIntosh, Calder, and Swift, 1976, p. 139).

over a large range of academic teaching their costs are lower than in the public sector.

In the light of demographic trends, official attitudes toward the division of responsibility in higher education have changed. The attempt in the mid-1960s to link the polytechnics more closely than the universities with the world of work and the application of knowledge has only partly succeeded. In science and technology, students have not been forthcoming to fill the available spaces in both the polytechnics and the universities. Increasingly (and disconcertingly) the polytechnics have filled their places with marginal students in the arts and social sciences, and the sharp reduction of teacher-training courses is likely to further increase the numbers in non-vocationally-oriented humanities. However, the most recent figures (1976 enrollments) show a significant rise among engineering entrants.

There will clearly be room within existing institutions in the mid-1980s for a large expansion of postsecondary education at an intermediate level. It should be government policy to encourage this expansion and to revive the idea of two-year courses for the new diploma in higher education, which could serve as either a terminal or an intermediate qualification. To promote two-year courses, it would almost certainly be necessary to relax the current 2 A level entry qualification attached to the diploma of higher education. There is also likely to be an increase in other two-year courses, and this expansion could precipitate the lengthening of the university first-degree course to four years (a development which many regard as inevitable sooner or later but discourage on financial grounds), establish formal credit links between two- and four-year courses, and make possible a new and integrated structure of two- and four-year institutions.

All of the above developments assume a continuing increase in the proportion of 18- to 24-year-olds remaining within the education system, full or part time, and therefore a continuing increase in the commitment of public funds to education. The latter is unlikely in the short and medium term but not necessarily out of the question in the long term.

If the logic of mass secondary education is carried through, both in terms of organization and curriculum, it will undoubtedly demand an extension of the range of postsecondary opportunities along some such lines as these. The pace at which this extension becomes explicit will be governed by the level of expansion that can be afforded at the upper level. It must be conceded that educational expansion is not currently a high priority for social policy makers in any political party or for senior administrators within the government service.

The Department of Education and Science has recently issued a discussion document (1978) giving high, medium, and low projections of students in higher education up to 1995–96. (These were not broken down between the university and non-university sectors.) The medium projection reflects the general demographic trend, peaking at 603,500 in 1985–86 and coming back to 519,500 in 1995–96. This projection assumes that the "age participation rate"—the proportion of the age group going on to higher education given the continuation of present entrance requirements—will rise from 13.5 percent in 1977–78 to 18.1 percent in 1995–96.

The policy issues addressed in the document concern the best ways to accommodate the expansion and subsequent contraction suggested by all the projections. Several strategies for minimizing costs and staffing problems are outlined in the form of a choice of policy responses.

Among ministers at the DES, there is preference for the strategy that would fill up vacant places in higher education by increasing opportunities for lower socioeconomic groups, women, and adult students.

Social Class and Educational Opportunity

In Britain, as in most European countries since the end of World War II, a principal objective of educational policy has been to extend access to education at all levels to all social classes, thereby broadening equality of opportunity generally. Exactly what equality of opportunity is, or exactly how it should be interpreted as a political goal, has been one of the burning arguments of the past 25 years; but nobody has disputed that a middle-class child has much better chances than a working-class child of staying on beyond the minimum school-leaving age, obtaining good school qualifications, and going on to higher education. It has been assumed that the disparity is too wide and that, by changing the system, it should be possible to make educational opportunities less dependent upon social background. How far has this been achieved? How far have the structural changes in the education system already described (not to mention the system of means-tested maintenance and fee grants available for students in higher education) succeeded in reducing the social imbalance in the upper reaches of the education system?

The research suggests that the social imbalance has been reduced somewhat, but it is the nature of educational reform that its effects cannot be measured for a full generation, and most of the evidence now available measures the effects of educational reform only up to the middle 1960s. It is not yet possible to show what the effect of the change in secondary school organization from separate, selective grammar schools and nonselective modern schools to comprehensive schools has been or will be when it is completed. In 1974, more than half the pupils from maintained schools who entered the universities still came from grammar schools that had not yet been absorbed into the new comprehensive system. It will be a good 10 years before any speculation about the effect of comprehensive reorganization on access to higher education can be based on hard evidence.

Some information about the social origins of students is collected annually by the Universities Central Council on Admissions. This can provide some indication of changing trends, but it does not cover the large sector of higher education outside the universities, for which statistics can only be collected through specific research projects. Such information as there is, therefore, really takes account only of the big postwar expansion of the grammar schools, the abolition of fees, and the first stage of expansion of postsecondary education.

The benchmark in much of the discussion is provided by the Glass study (1954), in particular Floud's analysis (1954) of the educational data assembled in 1949, measuring *inter alia* the educational record of groups of people born up to 1929. (A child born in 1929 reached the school-leaving age in 1943, and might—if not required to do National Service—go on to university in 1947–48 and graduate in 1951–52.)

The Glass study provided a social breakdown of boys entering grammar school between 1930 and 1941, of whom 40 percent were sons of professional and managerial parents, 20 percent of clerical and other nonmanual parents, and 40 percent of parents in manual occupations. In 1960, the Central Advisory Council for Education carried out its own survey on education between the ages of 15 and 18 (the Crowther Report). The survey included an investigation of the social composition of the cohort of boy grammar school entrants between 1946 and 1951 (that is, boys born between 1935 and 1940). The change in access in the 11 years between the period covered by the Glass study and the Crowther Report is shown in Table 20.

Table 20. Social origins of boys entering secondary
grammar schools before and after 1944,
England and Wales

	In percentage	
Occupations of fathers	*1930–41*	*1946–51*
Professional and managerial	40	26
Clerical and other nonmanual	20	18
Manual	40	56

Source: Glass, 1954, p. 129, Table vii; and Central Advisory Council for Education, 1960, p. 130, Table x.

On the basis of the Crowther figures, the professional and managerial group occupied one in four of the grammar school places, though they only numbered one in seven of the total population. The manual group, in contrast, comprised 77 percent of the population at large but only 56 percent of the grammar school population. These are figures for *entry* to grammar schools, and it must be borne in mind that the manual group tended to drop out of grammar school before age 18 in much larger numbers than the nonmanual group, so that working-class children were even more underrepresented at the top end of the school and in the university entrance group. By the time pupils reached the sixth-form level, about 55 percent came from nonmanual groups (Central Advisory Council for Education, 1954, p. 76).

The Report of the Committee on Higher Education (1963), known as the Robbins Report, continues the Crowther comparison by showing the extent of this social imbalance at the university level:

Table 21. Percentage of boys aged 18 in 1928–47 and
1960 entering university: by social class

		Percentage	
		Boys aged 18 in	
		1928–47[a]	*1960*[b]
Social class			
A.	Nonmanual	8.9	16.8
B.	Manual	1.4	2.6
C.	A-1 boys	3.7	5.8
	A divided by B	6.4	6.5

Survey of 21 year-olds

[a]Data for 1928–47 relate to England and Wales; data for 1960 to Great Britain. It is, however, reasonable to compare the two sets of figures, especially those in the bottom row.

[b]The data for 1960 were computed as follows: The percentage of all children aged 18 in 1960 who eventually enter university was assumed to be the same as the percentage of the age group who entered in that year (see Part IV, Table 33). The social-class distribution of those entering was assumed to be the same as for all male home undergraduates in 1961-62 (as shown in the Undergraduate Survey). The social-class distribution of the total age group was taken from the Survey of 21-year-olds.

Source: 1928–47–Floud, 1954, p. 137; 1960–Part IV, Table 33, U.G. Survey. Reproduced in Report of the Committee on Higher Education, 1963, Appendix I, Part II, p. 54, Table 15.

Additional statistics on university entrants' fathers' occupations are available from 1968 on from the Universities Central Council on Admissions. These are not strictly comparable with those used in the Robbins Report and only cover a short period, but they seem to bear more relation to the changing occupational structure within the community at large than to changes in social selection in the educational system.

Taken as a whole, these figures suggest what common sense also suggests—that wider access to education at all levels has most benefited those who were able to take advantage of it. Because English higher education started from such a narrow base, there were many capable students in the upper social groups in the prewar period who never went to university. The

**Table 22. Parental occupation of home candidates accepted
into university compared with census distribution:
October 1968 and October 1974**

Great Britain	*Percentages*			
Parent occupation	*Accepted candidates October 1968*	*Economically active males aged 45–59 1966 census*	*Accepted candidates October 1974*	*Economically active males aged 45–59 1971 census*
Administrative and managerial	14.0	6.0	15.0	7.0
Professional, technical, etc.	30.0	8.0	34.0	9.0
Other nonmanual	28.0	22.0	25.0	21.0
Manual and agricultural	28.0	64.0	26.0	62.0

Source: Universities Central Council on Admissions, 1967–68 and 1973–74.

first effect of broadening access has been to make extended education a much more widespread expectation for the sons (and to a growing extent, the daughters) of these already-privileged groups. The selective nature of the secondary school system—first through the mechanism of the grammar schools and later through the selective process still operated by examination options within the secondary course—provides a system that the offspring of middle-class families are better able to understand and to utilize than those whose traditional social expectation is to leave school at the earliest legal opportunity.

As the percentage entering higher education rises, the fraction of candidates who are drawn from the lower socioeconomic groups increases slowly until the threshold separating an elite system from a mass system is crossed. Britain is at present in the process of exploring this threshold at the secondary school level, but at the higher education level there is no suggestion that this threshold has yet been reached.

It is unlikely that within the next 10 years, the percentage of those entering higher education will exceed 25 percent of the age group. So long as that is so, there is no likelihood of any change in public policy that would radically redistribute access to higher education in such a way as sharply to reduce the opportunities of the advantaged section of the community and increase those of the less advantaged. It seems fairly clear that the speed with which secondary or higher education could change to provide more open access to opportunity is closely related to the development of the British economy generally and the functional needs of a society under severe industrial stress.

The elaborate system of means-tested grants for student maintenance and tuition fees has not operated as an effective method of equalizing access. It is arguable that without such a scheme there would be even fewer working-class students at the universities, but in practice the groups who gain admission to the universities and therefore become eligible for grants are already socially preselected and, notwithstanding the means test, much of the public money set aside for student grants goes to the sons and daughters of parents with better-than-average incomes. A recent government decision has somewhat increased this regressive effect by relieving the parents of all eligible home students of the payment of tuition fees, no matter what their income.

The principle of "to him that hath, shall be given" is further supported by the sharp division made between degree and degree-equivalent courses on the one hand and other postsecondary courses of a lower academic standard, including many professional and vocational courses, on the other. Degree courses carry "mandatory" awards: the local authorities are required by law to pay student fees and maintenance grants for such courses. But for other postsecondary students, grants are "discretionary": the local authority has the discretion to decide which to support and how much to pay, and in times of economic stringency (like the present) such discretionary payments are cut down severely. It so happens, of course, that the social composition of the two sets of students is likely to be different: those applying for mandatory awards will generally be drawn from families higher up the social scale than those who seek discretionary grants.

Educational Development and the World of Work

How, then, should we assess the results of 30 years of educational development since the end of World War II on young people growing up and entering the world of adulthood and work? Empirical and statistical evidence are notoriously unreliable with regard to such qualitative judgments, so we must turn to the complicated interrelationship between education and society that reflect the culture as a whole, and in which the tenuous link between educational development and social action is impossible to trace with any certainty.

The quantitative expansion of the education system has been reflected in a qualitative change in the jobs pursued by young men and women when they emerge from school or university. For most of the 30 years, employment has been remarkably buoyant, and the increase in the demand for higher skills (as a result of both technology and the upgrading of jobs formerly done by people without higher qualifications) has kept pace with the growth in the numbers of better educated people.

The resulting period of full employment has only recently ended. Which is the exception to the rule: the period of full employment (and low productivity growth and investment), which has been accepted as "normal" in the British postwar context; or the higher level of unemployment that has characterized the 1970s and threatens to continue over the medium term? While the period of full employment lasted, the education system seemed to mesh fairly well with employment, if only in the sense that young people were successfully absorbed and socialized. There is no proof that they were especially well prepared for work but, equally, there is no proof that they were not. Now that the postwar prosperity seems to have come to an end, however, critics have sought part of the cause of economic failure in the schools, universities, and colleges. They are almost certainly right to do so, in that the schools, like industry and business, provide cockpits where national neuroses can be observed: they encapsulate the cultural priorities and values which, in another context, are expressed in low productivity and bad industrial management and labor relations, no less than in more commendable aspects of life in modern Britain. A feature of the "great education debate" initiated by the prime minister's speech in October 1976 has been strong criticism of the education system as being out of touch with the world of work. A critique prepared by the Department of Industry, as part of an examination of constraints on economic growth, includes a general condemnation of the antitechnological, antiindustrial bias that distinguishes the English academic tradition. Sir Alex Smith, Director of the Manchester Polytechnic and Chairman of the Schools Council for Curriculum and Examinations (a body set up to oversee publicly supported curriculum development and advise the Secretary of State for Education and Science on examinations) has asked why Britain is so much better at getting Nobel prizes than at making and selling industrial products. Why has the rate of enrollments in social, administrative, and business studies in institutions of higher education gone up from 60,000 to more than 120,000 between 1965 and 1973, while numbers in engineering and technology steadily drifted downward during the same period? "These trends are alarming enough; yet if one looks more closely at the figures, some of the details are even more disturbing. Engineering and technology cover a range of subjects; within them production engineering is a study for which there is very little demand in view of its importance. In advanced courses in further education, for every new student enrolling in 1973 to study production engineering, there were five in economics, twelve in law, sixteen in sociology and forty in business and commerce" (Smith, 1976, p. 15). On the one hand, this trend reflects a decline in the relative importance of employment in manufacturing and a growth of employment in service (particularly public service occupations). In part, therefore, it represents the way in which the education system has responded to external factors, as it was bound to do. If the external environment—in employment, in social philosophy—had been different, so too would the choices of students and the growth areas in higher education. On the other hand, the enrollments also can be seen as the result of an increasingly irrelevant academic tradition, which gives pure science and research a higher status than applied science, technology, and production and which is oriented away from productive industry and toward the professions, the civil service, and the social services. This tradition is related to a history of elite education, once geared to the needs of a governing class and an overseas empire, which has never come to terms with the demands of manufacturing industry. Instead, it has enabled its educated elite to avoid manufacturing industry throughout their working lives and thereby enhance their own status.

It is difficult to influence directly such an educational tradition in a country where primary and secondary education administration is highly decentralized and where concepts of academic freedom inhibit any government intervention at the higher education level. One proposal is to create a range of government scholarships in technological subjects and the applied sciences, giving those who win them greater economic benefit than students on other grants. Another suggestion is to reorganize the whole student-grant system to give preferential treatment to students in disciplines with current technological applications. Action along these lines has not been taken because of the strong opposition this would arouse, particularly from the universities, but also because few people have confidence in the manpower-planning assumption built into any determined attempt to shift the balance of academic studies in this way. Within the total higher education budget, some funds have been made available at a few institutions to promote high-level science and technology courses in the area of management rather than research. The first students will enter these four-year courses (one year longer than the regular undergraduate course) at Birmingham; Imperial College, London; Strathclyde; and Manchester. Half their time will be devoted to engineering and the remainder divided between mathematics and management studies.

Such indirect methods of influencing student choices at the higher education level complement measures (referred to already) to encourage teachers to become better informed about industry, and, in particular, measures encouraging would-be teachers to gain some work experience in factories or offices before embarking on teacher training. This could be done by taking advantage of the present "buyers' market" for teachers, and making such experience a prerequisite for teacher training, or by the development of a vigorous program of in-service training undertaken jointly with industry.

What is obvious is that measures of the kind being discussed here, small in themselves, would only become important if they *reflected* a much larger change in the social climate. Such a social change would require a positive attitude toward the private sector within a mixed economy and toward the creation and enjoyment of wealth; it would also require teachers to hold up to their pupils a new and more favorable image of industry. Many people doubt that these attitudes reflect the current political climate in Britain, where conflict about industry is more evident than consensus and where political argument since the mid-1960s has been marked by ambivalence, which the schools have faithfully, if unconsciously, reflected. Some argue that this ambivalence has resulted in the undermining of the authority of the teachers and in what outsiders take to be a permissive attitude toward antisocial pupil behavior. Others link *this* to progressive attitudes toward competition in school—to the apparently misconceived antithesis between cooperation and competition on which much informal primary education is based—and to the unresolved arguments about setting, streaming (tracking), and mixed-ability grouping in the secondary school.

Education in England is noteworthy for the high degree of reliance placed on the independent professional judgment of the teachers. Because of the gradual introduction of the comprehensive secondary school, curricular controls on the primary schools have been progressively dismantled over a period of years. The primary schools have, therefore, been especially susceptible to trends in social science and educational philosophy that have transmitted the changing cultural mood. At the secondary level, the elitist tradition has ensured that practical subjects have been undervalued. The curricular revolution, which has gradually but effectively eroded this tradition, has not produced a confident, technological substitute. Moreover, early specialization—the three-year specialist university first degree— and the extent to which the universities have been excluded from professional training have all helped to perpetuate the idea that higher education is first and foremost a process of personal cultural enrichment and only secondarily a means of equipping people to play effective, wealth-creating roles in an industrial economy.

Just as universities have avoided professional training (with important exceptions such as the training of doctors), so too the schools have discarded their nineteenth-century functions with regard to vocational training. Any critical assessment of the past three decades of education must, therefore, ask if this dichotomy between general and vocational education has been beneficial. It is the logical outcome of the cultural background: vocational education had the lowest status; discarding it as a secondary school option was a means of gearing all secondary education to the more elitist educational assumptions of the favored sections of the school community. The dichotomy is also related to the growing power of the trade unions over craft skills (which, with shorthand and typewriting, form the basis of most vocational education, as the schools understand it) and the subordination of factory-level vocational training to the day-to-day pressures of industrial relations. In these circumstances, both trade unions and teachers wished to replace vocational education (which was often narrow and limiting) with watered-down forms of general education.

The result in the middle 1970s is a growing awareness that the secondary school curriculum needs to be overhauled but little unanimity on how this should be done. From the industrial side, there is a two-pronged argument for more attention to basic survival skills along with more attention to what the world of work is like. Now that industrialists are able to be more selective in their hiring, they complain bitterly about low standards. But industrialists are not alone in demanding better and more realistic education for those who are likely to enter employment straight from school at 16. Manpower economists see young people in competition for jobs with the people over 50 and with mature women. They regard greater general competence on the part of young people as being necessary if they are to get a fair share of such jobs as exist.

Both of these arguments have to be taken with a pinch of salt. The schools are likely to respond to the current pressure from industrialists and economists by tightening up and clamping down. Contrary to popular view, schools have always been concerned with basic competence, but in recent years the quest for methods of stimulating deprived, unmotivated urban pupils has sometimes obscured this fact. Schools will now become more conventional, and the curriculum will be pared down somewhat (perhaps to some advantage); but the problems of motivation and social control that have led to the educational developments—now interpreted by outsiders as fripperies and irrelevances—will remain. Only the most optimistic reactionary can really hope to reconstitute nonexistent good old days.

None of these predictions, however, answer the unresolved questions about vocational education. Is it possible to change the curricular diet of boys and girls at school so that they can actually learn skills that will help them to get a job and earn a living? Of course, better reading and arithmetic skills are likely to be useful in many jobs; but can the schools actually impart specific working techniques—as once, for example, a highly successful London trade school trained 13-year-olds in the craft of watchmaking? It is fairly clear that this is inconceivable in the present industrial context, where the union card as much as the technical skill identifies the craftsman and where technological change is, in any case, transforming training requirements. It is also impractical because, for a large proportion of boys and girls, there is no form of vocational education likely to be vocationally relevant: their employment expectations at best will take them into routine work for which four to eight weeks of on-the-job training is all that is required.

If a case for vocational education is to be made, therefore, it has to rest on more general grounds: on the idea that work is central to social life in a modern industrial society, and that vocational education may be a means of harnessing this fact to more general learning objectives. But vocational education on such terms as these becomes another motivational ploy to help resistant learners come to terms with their environment and with themselves and brings it back into mainstream arguments about education. It can hardly be doubted that if there is to be any serious attempt to extend the period of formal learning, either in full-time education or in the form of a mixture of employment, training, and education, progress will have to be made in this direction. Opponents of this view voice pessimism about work prospects in hard-pressed areas like the Northwest of England and Merseyside, insisting that survival skills in the present period include the resources needed to preserve self-respect and sanity in enforced idleness. "Education for unemployment" makes a poor slogan, but behind this poorly formulated notion lie questions about postindustrial society that challenge the concept of industrial employment as central to modern citizenship and, once again, plunge the education debate into the political and economic maelstrom. Any discussion of the present state of urban secondary schools, therefore, has to take place against this background.

There is a widespread belief that schools have become more tense and difficult, that teachers encounter much more aggressive hostility and verbal abuse and accept forms of hostile behavior as normal which would not have been tolerated in the early 1960s. There is a general acceptance that in many inner-city schools—London being the obvious example—an unacceptably large number of pupils are leaving school at 16 with poor standards of attainment in basic subjects, and that children from the West Indian community are strongly represented among those whose poor academic performance reflects their discouragement and despair over the youth employment problem.

There is little political support for the suggestion that the school-leaving age, which was raised to 16 in 1973–74, should be lowered; however, many would like to see a more flexible arrangement for pupils in their last year, who might be released from school, full or part time, into suitable forms of employment or work experience. Some limited schemes of release for work experience already exist under an education act of 1973, but only on a small scale. Teacher-opinion polls still show large minority support for the view that the decision to raise the school-leaving age was a mistake.

In other respects the formal education system, though in the process of being scourged by the current conservative backlash, is showing signs of recovering some confidence. Declining numbers of pupils and a smaller turnover of teachers combine to give the primary schools a greater stability. Having for years shown the ill effects of high staff turnover and a procession of young and inexperienced teachers, the primary schools are now in a better position to tackle their weaknesses than at any time since the end of the war.

5

Policies to Combat Youth Unemployment

Attempts by the government of the United Kingdom to intervene directly in the under-25 open labor market are recent and have for the most part been aimed at managing the supply of young workers. Measures designed specifically to stimulate demand for young workers have been meager in relation both to current youth unemployment levels and to the indirect impact of other public policies: deflationary fiscal and investment strategies; capital-intensive industrial modernization; regional planning; employee protection codes; and equal-opportunity legislation, which improves the competitive position of disadvantaged adult workers such as women and ethnic minorities.

Overall, the measures operated in the United Kingdom are similar to those adopted with varying emphasis in most of the other countries of the European Economic Community (EEC). They have evolved not as a comprehensively designed program but as a group of short-term, largely unrelated devices, intended to alleviate the effects of cyclical unemployment, superimposed on the established training and educational systems. Central government initiatives lean heavily on the activities already undertaken by local public authorities, voluntary agencies, and the industrial-training systems operated by both individual employers and by the government. Schemes of training and alternative work projects developed in these sectors are increasingly funded by central government and used as models by its agencies for their own large-scale interventions.

Some measures are not specifically aimed at young people but are intended to promote employment generally—for example, employment subsidies paid to employers to encourage them to take on or retain staff and early-retirement schemes aimed at creating vacancies by offering income support to workers in their sixties. Among the measures more specifically affecting young people are the following:

• *Alternative employment projects,* which reduce pressure on the labor market by providing gainful occupations—normally for a limited term—for a significant proportion of the young unemployed;

• *Full-time training courses,* which defer the entry of school leavers into the labor market and improve their qualifications, or remove older adolescents from the market for a time, or equip them with skills which are in demand;

• *Full-time work experience,* occupying the same role but confined to those who have had no experience of employment since leaving school;

• *Further-education courses,* provided under special arrangements for those out of work;

• *Subsidized craft training,* either carried out by employers or provided under the auspices of industrial training boards, and intended to maintain the intake of apprentices and other trainees during economic recession;

• *Vocational preparation,* for those in the lower years of the age group who are currently employed, aimed at increasing their general skills and effectiveness as workers (as well as producing other personal development), thereby improving their prospects of retaining their jobs or securing other posts in competition with adults;

• *Strengthening of the youth employment services,* intended to secure a better matching of jobs and applicants, and to optimize the use by the age group of the whole range of facilities and opportunities available.

The bulk of this activity, especially the portion directly funded by central government, has been initiated since the spring of

1975. It has absorbed a considerable part of the £800 million provided to keep jobs open, support training, or stimulate industrial expansion in Great Britain and Northern Ireland.

Earlier Measures

Interventions in the youth labor market that occurred before 1975 were mainly the by-product of government measures aimed at other objectives or sponsored by bodies outside central government. The measure with the most impact on the supply of adolescent labor was the raising of the school-leaving age from 15 to 16 in 1974. Although the objectives of the measure were broadly educational and social, it had a marked effect both in the short and in the longer term. Industry found itself deprived of its normal intake of school leavers in the first year after the change, and it is thought that the adjustments many employers made at that time permanently removed a number of posts for workers under 18 from the general stock.

A further effect, increasingly manifested as other factors narrowed the job opportunities for 16-year-olds, was the tendency for more pupils to stay on voluntarily beyond the compulsory leaving age. This, in turn, reduced the supply of suitable recruits for many apprenticeship schemes with maximum recruitment age. Also in 1974, the provisions of a 1973 education act enabling state schools to release pupils for limited spells of work experience in industry came into force. Together with the professionalization of the youth careers advisory services—now reorganized as a wing of the education service operated by local authorities—these provisions laid the foundation for systematic educational attempts to improve the employability of young people.

During the early 1970s, a number of voluntary agencies, in particular those dealing with disadvantaged adolescents, experimented with small-scale projects designed to provide paid occupation for those who could not find work. Funded partly by charitable contributions, but often with subsidies from the local-authority youth services, they produced a number of models for the creation of work outside the normal labor market. Often the projects were aimed either wholly or partly at groups who needed remedial help, such as truants and delinquents; thus they emphasized a training or educational component. Among the more enduring of the formulas developed in this way was the "youth workshop," in which groups of youngsters learned to cooperate in the production of simple goods or services. One valuable by-product of these attempts to provide work was the provision of personal and career counseling to young people who would otherwise have been entirely divorced from the help of the voluntary and statutory youth services.

The largest of the projects to emerge at this time was Community Industry (CI), sponsored by the National Association of Youth Clubs. Set up in the winter of 1971, it operates a network of enterprises throughout Britain providing various goods and services to the community which would not normally be supplied by commercial industry. Young people working in the projects have the status of ordinary employees and are paid wages: they are expected to turn out work that meets the economic and quality criteria of the users, who are mainly local authorities and community groups. Some of the young people are assigned to craft or educational courses during their employment. The scheme is administered by a national management board representing the clubs, the Trades Union Congress, the Confederation of British Industries, and the Department of Employment. The wage cost of the young workers and of the 500 or so adult staff who run CI is funded directly through the department, unlike most of the other youth employment and training schemes, whose funds are channeled through the Manpower Services Commission. Local authorities provide sites and equipment. Entry to CI projects is limited to those under 18, who nominally spend a year or more with the undertaking. Local-authority career officers are closely involved both in recruitment and supervision of the youths.

Stimulating Labor Demand

The main way in which the U.K. government has attempted in recent years to increase the total stock of jobs available, or to modify the pattern of job-market contraction, is by the selective use of industrial investment grants. Some £300 million was made available in 1975 and 1976 for expansion, modernization, and regional development and for the acceleration of capital schemes already projected. The principal effect of such inducements is likely to be long term, although some immediate demand for labor in the construction and equipment industries may also have resulted. The net significance of such grants for future youth employment must be assessed in the light of:

1. the total industrial modernization strategy, with its heavy emphasis on the objective of reduced manning (a good example being the publicly owned steel industry);

2. the fact that additional demands for labor are distributed over all working-age groups, and because most modernization schemes reduce the relative requirement for unskilled and short-term workers, the distribution is likely to be less favorable to adolescents than in the past;

3. the emphasis on channeling new investment into manufacturing rather than into the distribution and service operations, which have traditionally provided a high proportion of the total market for youth labor.

Within the overall use of selective investment grants, there has been a minor attempt to encourage the kind of labor-intensive developments that are likely to replicate the traditional mix of age groups in the work force; the scale of these efforts is exemplified by the £1 million (out of the total of £300) allocated in 1976 for the construction of small factories in rural areas.

Not surprisingly, these long-term measures lack any attempt to ensure that the new capital projects make a specific contribution to the demand for youth labor; this is consistent with the attitude that youth unemployment is almost entirely a cyclical variable. It was not until the end of 1976 that this assumption began to be questioned publicly, albeit hesitantly, by the government's own advisers in the Manpower Services Commission. However, short-term measures to alleviate the effects of the economic crisis of the mid-1970s, in accord with this overall government view, have been based on the need to stimulate or preserve the demand for young workers or simply to reallocate unemployment by changing the relative chances of different groups. The devices employed have included differential subsidies to employers and inducements to (or pressures on) older staff to retire earlier than they otherwise would. Additional measures have been designed to maintain the general stock of jobs for all age groups and to improve the matching of vacancies and applicants.

Employment Subsidies

The Temporary Employment Subsidy was one unemployment countermeasure introduced in 1975 to help firms in those parts of the country designated "assisted areas" to defer layoffs due to obsolescence. Covering all age groups, the scheme was at first restricted to firms planning to lay off 50 or more staff; they were offered a subsidy of £10 a week for a maximum of three months for each post retained. Subsequent modifications increased the payment to £20 a week, reduced the minimum qualifying requirement to 10 layoffs, and extended the scheme to cover all private employers throughout Britain. By the 1977 budget, when the scheme was again modified and its duration extended to one year, subsidies had been paid for the retention of 224,000 workers, of whom about 10 percent were under age 21.

The Temporary Employment Subsidy affected, of course, only those who were already in employment. A few weeks after its introduction, at the beginning of the 1975–76 school year, the government announced a measure designed primarily to help those who had left school at the end of the previous term and had not yet found lasting employment. Employers who hired school leavers with six weeks or less of employment were to be paid £5 per youth for the first 26 weeks. Employers were debarred from claiming both subsidies for one employee, and school leavers could not be recruited to displace existing workers. In the 12-month life of the scheme, more than 30,000 school leavers benefited from it.

In September 1976 a replacement scheme was announced—the Youth Employment Subsidy. A good deal more flexible than its predecessor, it applied to anyone under 20 who had been continuously registered as unemployed for six months;

and because it was payable for any period between 8 and 26 weeks, it could be used to subsidize short-term employment.

The subsidy of £10 a week was payable to nationalized industries and private employers but not to other public service administrations or to voluntary agencies. In the first six months of the scheme, about 10,000 applications were approved, a considerably lower rate of take-up than had been provided for in the £5.4 million budget; nevertheless, the scheme was among measures whose extension was announced in the March 1977 budget.

Early Retirement

Pressures on staff to retire before the maximum age, either voluntarily or under compulsory procedures, increased during 1976, both in branches of the central government civil service and in local government administration. The pressures arose from a drive to cut staffs in absolute terms (rather than by any overt intention to change the age profile) and were in most cases strongly resisted by the trade unions. In the case of the bigger civil-service unions, this was one of the principal issues leading to union refusals to cooperate in work-experience schemes for the young unemployed. However, the retirement rate was clearly related in practice to the ability of agencies to recruit young people within the governing economic constraints, particularly since even one-for-one replacement offers significant savings where, as in these public services, the pay structure is incremental.

In September 1976, the Department of Employment announced a limited scheme to encourage some workers to retire in favor of young unemployed. The Job Release Scheme offered men of 64 and women of 59—that is, a year below their respective retirement ages—a tax-free allowance of £23 a week—payable until the date on which they were normally due to retire—if they gave up their jobs and were replaced by one of the registered unemployed. Also eligible for the allowance were those equally close to retirement age but unemployed, who could claim the benefit if they contracted not to work during the period for which it was available. The scheme, which came into effect at the beginning of 1977, operated only in designated assisted areas and has covered about 20,000 workers, of whom about half were previously unemployed. This has created a few additional spaces for young workers, although probably fewer than originally envisaged.

Employment Services and Moving Allowances

There is a wide range of government grants to help workers meet the costs of searching for work or taking jobs at a distance from home. The grants include reimbursement of fares to attend an interview and temporary separation allowances and rehousing grants (which can, in some circumstances, exceed £2,000) for those moving to new jobs. These grants apply to all age groups, and the only discernible provision relating especially to young workers is a rule that limits those under age 18 to only four assisted visits home, compared with the twelve to which older people are entitled. The main positive provision for young workers takes the form not of grants but of special placement counseling and selection facilities.

Occupational selection courses are run by the Training Services Agency for 16- to 18-year-olds who are undecided about what kind of work to seek. In addition to identifying vocational aptitudes, the courses, which last between 6 and 13 weeks, offer broad life and social skills training; they normally serve as a prelude to specific craft training either on TSA courses or in industry. Trainees receive a tax-free allowance on a scale which, at the beginning of 1977, offered 16-year-olds a minimum of £13.65 a week.

The main facilities for seeking and finding work, however, are provided through the Careers Service, which is entirely responsible for the placement of school leavers below the age of 18 and, in general, handles those in older age groups for the first two years after they leave full-time education. The responsibility for those under age 25 as a whole, therefore, is shared between the Careers Service and the MSC's Employment Services Agency, the national service responsible for adult recruitment and placement. The demarcation between the activities of the two bodies in relation to the placement of 18- to 25-year-olds is not a matter of statutory definition but a loose working arrangement between them. The Careers Service has existed in its present form since 1974. Reference has already been made to the legislation that reorganized the whole structure of government-funded manpower and training services. The youth section of the Department of Employment's placement services was merged with the careers advice departments already run by most local authorities as part of their educational provision. These new careers departments became an integral part of the local-authority-administered educational service; but whereas the authorities were responsible to the Department of Education and Science for the main part of their education function, the Department of Employment was responsible for overseeing their careers work.

In addition to their key statutory role of maintaining the school-leaver unemployment register, receiving notifications of vacancies, and handling placement, the careers departments are involved in a wide range of other interventions in the youth employment field, either directly as counselors, or indirectly as coordinators, communicators, and agents of access between young people, the education service, industry, and others concerned in the training and alternative work programs described below.

Because the service is administered by local authorities and its expenditure controlled by them, there is considerable variation in the level and range of activity undertaken in different areas of the country. This is partly a function of differences in staffing levels, and in order to help reduce this uneven allocation of resources, since 1975 the Department of Employment has begun to fund directly the appointment of a limited number of additional officers in the local-authority departments. Some concern was expressed in the national advisory council at the beginning of 1977 that this step had not been as effective as might have been hoped in evening up services; it was thought that a few of the less active authorities had taken advantage of the directly funded appointments to reduce their own expenditure on staff.

The basis on which local-authority expenditure is funded strictly limits the amount of direct executive action the central government can take. This has a bearing on the development of policy with regard to vocational education and training and the provision of career education and career advice. In particular, it affects activities in which there is no mandatory level of provision, such as courses for those who have left the school system.

The local authorities have wide discretion under the law to decide the level of service they will provide, so long as they meet whatever statutory duties are laid upon them, such as ensuring suitable educational facilities for children of school age. In principle, since they are also empowered to levy certain local property taxes, they are free to decide what their expenditures will be. However, a major part of each local-authority expenditure now comes from central exchequer funds, paid in the form of a grant to each authority (known as the Rate Support Grant). The annual grant is determined by calculating the level of provision the local authorities as a whole are expected to make in each of the principal services they administer—education, social services, highways, and so on—but no attempt is made to police the actual use of the funds. The central government may issue guidelines setting forth its priorities, but in the end local authorities make their own budgets and do not regard the block grant as made up of fixed components. In periods of retrenchment—and particularly when many local authorities are becoming anxious about the inflation of local tax rates—spending on one or more services may be cut back to substantially below the levels envisaged by the central government. Thus, while one may talk of the total sum that government intends to be spent on the Careers Service, it is not possible to ascertain exactly how much has actually been spent.

The role of the Careers Service in youth employment measures and in the developing complex of traditional educational facilities had become so important by 1976 that the government sought to protect it from the economies that local authorities were obliged to make in other parts of the education service. Thus for 1977–78 it increased the provision for careers work in the grant it made to local authorities to £24 million, a figure that assumed the authorities together would spend about

£35 million, which would allow for a 3 percent growth in the service.

Training Posts

Steps taken to expand industrial-training programs since 1975 have substantially affected the number of training places offered by employers and thus the short-term demand for youth labor. It is often argued that in the longer term all training measures should be seen as means of influencing the demand for youth labor both by improving the competitive position of the age group in the general market and by contributing eventually to national economic growth. Any government-sponsored alternative to unemployment is bound to provide some kind of experience likely to enhance employability. The measures undertaken in the training field are examined below, together with those other programs whose principal effect in the short term has been to withdraw significant numbers of young people from the labor market.

Job Creation Program (JCP). Derived from ideas first tried out in the United States in the 1960s (the New Careers experiments) and developed on a larger scale in Canada, the Job Creation Program has sought in essence to provide—at appropriate normal wage rates (subject to a maximum)—various kinds of work that benefit the community by improving the environment or by contributing to the solution of social and community problems. The interpretation of "community benefit" is wide enough to embrace some kinds of work within trade-union and political organizations, but it firmly excludes activities that produce commercial profit or are otherwise carried out by normal labor.

The government made it plain to the MSC that priority should be given to the young unemployed and their training requirements and, in the choice of projects, to urban renewal. It envisaged that the ability of the commission to defray wage costs would persuade a variety of local bodies—including private employers and voluntary organizations, local government, and the nationalized industries—to sponsor and run the projects. Ten area offices were set up by the commission to administer the scheme; the authorization of projects, however, was made the responsibility not of officials but of lay committees representing local employers, unions, and local authorities and headed by an independent chairman (usually a person of high standing in the academic community).

Because it was seen as an urgently required first-aid measure and was announced at a time when unprecedented high unemployment was producing acute political and union pressures, the JCP was brought into operation with considerable haste. There was an obvious temptation to concentrate activity on the most readily identifiable group of potential sponsors, the local authorities, who were known to have the management and physical resources at hand and might be best placed to suggest projects of community benefit. For the first six months, the program was largely dominated by local-authority-sponsored projects. Subsequently, however, an increasing proportion of the projects came to be sponsored by voluntary organizations, including the biggest of the ventures, a series of projects run in Sunderland by Community Service Volunteers, which provided work for about 250 adolescents in hospitals, community and youth centers, nursery schools, and old people's homes. The strict exclusion of profit-yielding projects, however, meant in practice that the response from either private employers or the nationalized industries remained almost negligible.

By the beginning of 1977, some 72 percent of all the projects had been sponsored by local authorities and other public bodies, with voluntary agencies running another 10 percent; these overall figures were heavily weighted by the early months, during which local authorities alone had sponsored 85 percent. By March 1977, the U.K. budget expenditure on the JCP had grown to £105 million and had provided a total of 75,000 jobs of an average duration of 31 weeks. The commission had fixed a maximum life of 12 months for projects, but in practice those that proved effective were normally extended; thus in effect the maximum limited only the length of time that an individual could be employed. One-third of the projects were concerned with the improvement of land features; 15 percent were concerned with construction tasks; 21 percent involved some kind of artistic, educational, or information activity; 17

percent dealt with the social and health services; and 10 percent were research or survey studies. Nearly 15 percent of all projects were located in inner-city areas.

A survey of former JCP employees in five areas undertaken by the MSC in September 1976 (MSC, 1977) convinced the commission that the program was reaching its main target group of the unqualified and untrained under age 25. It showed that the majority of those participating had left school at the earliest opportunity and that nearly two-thirds of them had no educational qualification. Although 60 percent of the whole group had worked since leaving school, this was true of only 30 percent of those under age 18. The majority said they had benefited from their JCP participation, mentioning either the general experience of work or of a particular skill, responsibility, and the fact that they had been kept active. There was general (but not universal) satisfaction with the supervision of the projects. The main criticism of the scheme—made by the trade unions (including the National Union of Teachers), by voluntary organizations, and by individual young people at conferences—are that the short-term nature of the employment and of the whole scheme limits the development of project content and the ability of the projects to provide anything of lasting value. A complaint that has been voiced a good deal by individuals and radical groups—and indeed by some local careers officers—is that the scheme simply takes people off the dole and returns them to it after a brief respite. The general secretary of the Trades Union Congress stated that it was intended to do precisely that. His phrase was "It's better than nowt."

The MSC 1976 validation survey data suggest that there are some lasting advantages attached to participation. About one-fifth of those in JCP left to take a job during the project; nearly half found work soon after completing their term with the program. The median wage among those who found work was £29 per week, compared with a median of £27 among those who were at work before joining the JCP. (The median wage in the JCP itself was £24.) However, the difference in median wage rates before and after JCP experience might in part be accounted for by a general rise in wage rates during the time when those involved in the JCP were out of the labor market.

A criticism that has been made both by the British Youth Council and by teacher organizations is the lack of training provided for the majority of the participants. The National Union of Teachers (NUT) has suggested that 77 percent of the projects provided no visible training component; the British Youth Council alleged that, despite the employment of more than 1,400 young teachers, most of them in a nonteaching role, 60 percent of the projects offered no more than on-the-job training, itself frequently barely existent. However, while the council implied that the teachers within the JCP should more often be used to provide active instruction, the NUT expressed dismay at their being used in any kind of teaching role, which it felt should be carried out by more experienced staff secured from the school system. In its March 1977 report on youth unemployment, the council estimated that only 15 percent of the projects had entailed any form of off-the-job training, which had been more difficult to provide as a result of financial cuts in the further-education colleges.

The MSC's own validation survey provided some evidence of a conflict of perspectives on training: 70 percent of the projects in which survey respondents had worked were throught to provide on-the-job training and 10 percent of the projects included day release; only 1 in 10 did not set out to provide any kind of instruction. But more than 70 percent of the respondents said that they themselves had received no training.

There has also been some complaints from voluntary organizations and statutory youth services staff of considerable disparity in the criteria adopted by the area action committees. The MSC had, however, accepted the risks of inconsistency and inequity inherent in a decentralized program for the sake of flexibility, participative democracy, and responsiveness to specific local needs and resources (and also, perhaps, because it was sensitive to accusations of bureaucratic centralism).

Work Experience Program (WEP). The 1973 Education Act provided for limited work experience as a kind of reverse day release for pupils in the latter part of their school career. The extension since then of the concept to include a full-time post-school program has been a potent source of confusion—not least to the young people involved.

The Work Experience Program, which has been operated since the autumn of 1976 by the MSC, is aimed at a subgroup within the same group of young people that has been the principal target of the JCP. The WEP was announced as part of a new set of unemployment countermeasures at a time when school-leaver unemployment had reached a record seasonal level; £19 million were allocated to provide for placement of unemployed young workers under age 19 in industrial or commercial enterprises for six months or more to gain experience of working life. They were to be neither employees nor trainees in the normal sense, although the program emphasized the need for a planned and properly supervised program of induction and subsequent training, including, whenever possible, formal instruction in general skills, either by day release for further education or through existing in-company and training-board facilities. The commission would pay the young people a flat rate, free of tax or social security contributions, of £16 a week, which was of the same order as the grants payable under many of the commission's other training programs and somewhat below the medium take-home pay in the Job Creation Program.

The terms and context in which the secretary of state for employment announced the new program made plain that whatever its merits as an innovation in transitional education, the principal justification for launching it at that time was the contribution it would make to removing a further 60,000 young workers from the labor market during the following 12 months. The fact that the program was regarded primarily as a temporary crisis expedient was underlined by the time limits initially set for it: rather than allowing sufficient time to gain acceptability among the employers, whose cooperation was essential, the program was sanctioned to operate only until the following September, which meant that applications would close in March. It was estimated that some 30,000 young workers might be placed during that period. As was the case of the JCP, access was through the Careers Service, except for those who had left school more than two years earlier, who applied through the

Commission's Employment Services Agency, which provided placement services for the adult labor market as a whole. The commission itself was to seek the places, inviting applications from employers through six area teams.

As it turned out, applications were very slow in coming in, and by the end of 1976, the target was revised downward to 20,000. Subsequently, and after some intensive publicity, interest among employers began steadily to grow. Whereas 68 percent of the first 4,000 places to be approved had been in the service industries (mainly the distributive trades), manufacturing and extractive industry together accounted for only 20 percent. The share taken by major companies was not as large as had been expected: with one or two significant exceptions, such as Imperial Chemical Industries and Chrysler, the only large organizations to show interest were the retail chains, and this may partly explain why in the first months more than 60 percent of the placements were girls. The majority of the projects continued to be operated by firms with less than 500 staff, although more places came to be offered in manufacturing. In February 1977, when the secretary of state agreed to extend the scheme for a further four months, it was within sight of its revised target, with the rate of applications still growing.

As a measure to relieve youth unemployment by removing a substantial number of young workers from the labor market for a limited period, the Work Experience Program may be seen as a more sophisticated, second-generation device, serving largely the same purposes as job creation. In that role, like the JCP, it pays young workers from central government funds to engage full time in an occupation that is only incidentally productive of goods or services, but is not primarily training in a defined skill area. However, in contrast to the mixed and ambivalent attitudes which the JCP has elicited, the WEP appeared from its early stages to win something close to universal approval. Unions, teachers, youth organizations, professionals of the Careers Service, and the often self-critical staff of the commission itself grew increasingly enthusiastic about both the concept and the way in which it was being implemented. Training managers in participating companies spoke glowingly of their experience with the first groups of young workers placed with them, and some admitted that it was leading to a change in the attitude of their managements towards the recruitment of school leavers. While the commission and the careers officers, through whom the applicants were channeled, continued to stress that work experience contained no implied offer of a job with the host company, there was nothing to prevent companies from recruiting the youth as permanent staff, and from the earliest months of the scheme a number did so. The development was observed with some reservations by the unions, who were concerned that some companies might use work experience as a means of bringing in recruits on probation, sidestepping the provisions of employee-protection legislation. It was unlikely, however, that the unions would press the issue unless there were clear signs that companies were deliberately using the process as a substitute for their normal methods of recruitment.

What has won approval for the Work Experience Program more than any other factor is that it is predicated on the need to provide lasting benefits for those participating. Its primary purpose in the eyes of the MSC is to facilitate transition from school to work and to provide young people with some understanding of the work environment and its realities before they choose a career. The seriousness with which the commission regards this scheme as an educative process is manifest in its concern that the experience for each participant be planned and supervised and include a training component. A random survey carried out by the MSC in the first weeks of the program showed that 10 percent of the projects contained a significant content of further education and that 16 percent of those participating were either studying on day release or receiving formalized in-company training. Subsequently the commission allocated £100,000 to fund further education courses in local-authority colleges specifically for WEP trainees. The commission prepared its own "life and social skills" syllabus and trained its own instructors to help employers to initiate courses in this field to undertake the instruction directly. The whole approach that the commission brought to the Work Experience

Program from its inception indicated that, whatever the circumstances under which it was launched, the MSC saw it as a long-term contribution to transitional education that would outlast the need to combat cyclical unemployment.

"Pump-priming workshops" and the Clerical Training Awards.
Two smaller programs have developed as variants of the Job Creation Program and the Work Experience Program. In 1976, the Department of Employment sanctioned the allocation of 1 percent of the JCP budget to the funding of "pump-priming workshops." Unlike the mainstream JCPs, these commission-supported projects were intended to become permanent, viable enterprises producing goods or services, usually run on a cooperative basis.

Their problem, commercially, was that they started out with the costs of a work force and then had to find ways of earning sufficient revenue to stay in business, covering overhead even during the period when the program was paying their wage costs. By the beginning of 1977, about 50 workshop projects had been approved.

The Clerical Training Awards Scheme was a sister project to the WEP, devised by the MSC in the late summer of 1976 as a means of providing for unemployed young people in the same age group a combination of work experience and skills training which would equip them for clerical work. Work experience in offices was, indeed, available under the WEP itself; but the specialized scheme aimed to provide more specific training in clerical skills leading to a formal qualification. It was also seen as an opportunity for the local authorities to make a contribution, as a group of large employers, to the new measures for helping the young unemployed.

Under the scheme, financed by the commission's Training Services Agency (TSA) and administered through the Local Government Training Board, the larger local authorities, for the most part those that controlled educational facilities, were asked to provide a one-year course for unemployed prospective clerical workers. They were expected to recruit the participants in their own localities and offer them both practical training within civic departments and day-release studies in local colleges and institutions. The studies, where possible, would lead to the Certificate in Office Studies. For the duration of the course, the TSA would provide students with a £17-a-week grant. The agency would also fully reimburse the authorities for the costs they incurred in recruitment, provision of courses, and administration.

The program did not get off to a good start. The TSA was forced to launch the scheme in a rush early in 1977 in circumstances that were not particularly auspicious. At that time, the Civil Service Department was still trying to persuade the unions to agree to the introduction of the Work Experience Program in central government departments; the civil service unions, resentful of the staffing cuts being made as part of a major program of public economies, were refusing to allow even the MSC to take WEP trainees into its own offices. There was reason to suppose that there would be similar problems in some areas in getting union cooperation for the proposed clerical scheme.

In Northern Ireland, where political and economic imperatives brought about active government intervention in the labor market earlier than in the rest of Great Britain, certain other programs have been introduced alongside these schemes. Enterprise Ulster runs construction projects of community benefit in which unemployed workers—adults and youths—work and train for regular jobs, most of which will be in the construction industry. Over 15 percent of the 1,700-member work force is under age 20. Integrated work force units are similar in concept to the JPC pump-priming workshops; groups of about a dozen unskilled workers are trained in complementary skills so that they can eventually form an effective production unit, which may become the basis of a viable commercial enterprise.

Training Scheme Incentives

The various measures introduced to maintain, extend, and expand the training effort cover a diverse range of training objectives, but the twin need to stimulate the recruitment of young trainees into industry and to remove other young workers from the labor market largely dictated the timing of these measures and was the main justification for allocating large resources at a time of rapid retrenchment in other public expenditures. The one area of innovation to which this did not apply was vocational preparation for those already at work, which was embarked on when the need for countercyclical measures was thought to be diminishing. In addition to steps to maintain and increase training places within industry and selection courses, four separate training programs have been set up by the Training Services Agency.

Training Opportunities Scheme (TOPS). This scheme was introduced primarily to provide retraining for employed adult workers. Although a number of special courses have been mounted for unemployed school leavers, often in areas where there are specific local problems or requirements, the majority of the 600 courses that had become available by 1977 were for men and women over age 19; entry was restricted to workers who had been away from full-time education for three years or more and had not taken part in any government-funded training in the previous five years. The courses were open both to the unemployed and those already working who wanted to acquire new skills. TOPS training was available at nearly 1,000 establishments throughout Britain—including the 50 "skill centers"— training centers run directly by the TSA itself—colleges of further education, or on employers' premises. All together, these establishments offered a wide variety of craft courses, operator training, and short courses intended to adapt existing skills to new applications.

Those accepted for the courses received tax-free allowances based on an age scale and providing for dependents and traveling expenses. In the first two years of the scheme the emphasis was on expansion, and courses were initiated for virtually every identifiable need, providing a total of 80,000 places. In 1977, when it was clear that the scheme was firmly established and would have no difficulty in achieving its target numbers, the program became more selective, and the range of courses offered was more closely related to the existing and forecast needs of industry.

Short industrial courses. These three-month courses were intended to provide general skills that would qualify trainees to embark on semiskilled or clerical employment. They were normally oriented toward a particular occupation and frequently included instruction in life and social skills, particularly those related to finding and keeping a job. The courses were run either in colleges or on employers' premises.

Wider opportunities courses. These courses were aimed at young workers whom the Careers Service or the Employment Services Agency considered hamstrung by lack of motivation. Lasting up to 24 weeks, they were intended to help the young people to find out what sort of work they liked and were suited for and to build up the confidence and desire to embark on training or to tackle a job.

Preparatory courses. These were virtually courses of remedial education, provided at further-education colleges to provide basic skills for those unable to read simple instructions or make simple calculations of the type required either in general employment or to meet the entry requirements of TOPS courses. The length of the courses was matched to individual needs, running for a maximum of three college terms. The normal minimum age of entry was 19, the same as for general TOPS courses; but with immigrants in mind it was relaxed to admit unemployed young people over age 17 who had been living outside the U.K. for a year or more while of British statutory school age.

Local-Government and Other Public-Service Interventions

In addition to the countrywide measures sponsored or funded by the Department of Employment and the Manpower Services Commission, a great variety of initiatives has been undertaken independently by local authorities in various parts of the United Kingdom. Work preparation courses, literacy and arithmetic instruction, and alternative work projects have been begun by local education departments, usually involving the Careers Service or the statutory youth services, and often in cooperation with employers in the area. Individual further-education colleges, particularly in the period before the Training Services

Agency had become fully established as a major funder of work-related courses, put on special courses to help unemployed youth and those educationally disadvantaged.

Some city authorities have obtained substantial funds under the central government's provisions for urban aid to establish courses for specific groups of young people, such as those belonging to ethnic minorities. The Community Relations Commission, a government agency, has encouraged and assisted in these initiatives. There is also evidence that some local authorities, despite powerful pressures from the central government to reduce expenditures, deliberately set out to create a number of additional posts within their permanent services for young workers at the peak of cyclical unemployment.

Government Intervention Beyond 1977

As we have seen, by 1977 the U.K. government and its agencies—together with local authorities, the education service, and voluntary organizations—had become responsible for a wide assortment of interventions in the youth labor market. The range of measures operating has been progressively introduced on an ad hoc basis as various needs were identified, as pressures grew to act in a particular area, or because new solutions were offered by groups and organizations. The situation produced by this ad hoc process was increasingly criticized by voluntary agencies and teacher associations, among others, who pointed to the patchiness of the provision, overlapping of courses, and inconsistencies both in funding criteria for different activities and in allowances paid to young people participating in the various programs. More urgently, the critics pointed out, despite the very high total of resources committed to the activities, they did not succeed in providing constructive activity for all, or even the majority, of school leavers who were unable to obtain work on the open labor market.

By the middle of 1976, the major youth organizations in particular had begun to press for a comprehensive youth-opportunity program that would offer everyone up to age 18 who could not find a job some form of education, training, or paid work. They urged that the program have an integrated career and consistent structure that would relate to the long-term needs of those currently in their teens as well as to the future requirements of the community and the economy. By the end of the year, the MSC accepted the desirability of providing an integrated and comprehensive program if its feasibility could be established. In the autumn, a working party was set up under a senior MSC executive, Geoffrey Holland, to examine the feasibility of offering a universal guarantee of the kind that the youth bodies were urging. Because most of the current provision for unemployed young workers was funded under the government's short-term countercyclical measures, which might be allowed to lapse if there were any substantial improvement in the economy during 1977, the working party was required to complete its recommendations with dispatch.

The government committed itself to the Holland working party's proposals on June 29, 1977. These proposals are: £18 per week, including travel expenses, will be paid to those under age 19 participating. The only condition imposed is that unemployed young people will have to wait six weeks before they qualify for a place. In addition, there will be a Special Temporary Employment Program (STEP) to provide up to 12 months of work for those over age 19. The new STEP scheme will add 25,000 places and will concentrate on groups hard hit by the current recession in areas of heavy unemployment. The new scheme will also provide 8,000 places for unemployed adults to act as supervisors and instructors on work-experience projects. The JCP will be extended until the end of 1977 when it will be replaced.

There was nothing really new in the opportunities recommended for jobless youngsters. But the working party believed that the proposals broke new ground in their scope and comprehensiveness: no Western government had as yet attempted to intervene in the youth labor market on such a scale or as purposively.

The new MSC program was essentially a range of training or work-experience options, all of them of the kind already operated in the U.K. and in other countries, either as short-term devices to relieve pressure on the job market or as part of work force retraining programs. The commission, drawing on its own experience and that of the voluntary agencies, attempted to assemble a rational package of opportunities calculated to meet the needs of the different ability groups among those jobless under age 19 and to provide a constructive progression of experiences for those unable to obtain work after completing one kind of project or training course. The program proposed two main kinds of opportunity: courses designed to prepare young people for work and different kinds of work experience (Figures 12 and 13).

The availability of specific options from within this total range in each area of the country would be decided by a committee representing local civic, educational, community, management, and trade-union interests and would vary with local and seasonal needs. A wide range of choice is needed, said the commission, "because no single remedy is appropriate . . . . Young people object to being regimented" (MSC, 1977, p. 33).

An important principle in the scheme is the single flat-rate allowance—not varying with age, activity, or location—which was proposed for all participants. The figure suggested was £18 a week, normally to include travel expenses, although it was envisaged that where these were excessive there should be some additional payment. The idea of a standard allowance was that it would prevent money considerations from becoming a factor in participants' choice of options and would also facilitate free movement between different parts of the program, which the commission considered an essential part of its concept. The program was to be open to all those who had left full-time education and had not yet reached their nineteenth birthday, but was funded on the basis of providing for a maximum of 234,000 young people a year, only one-half of the commission's own forecast of what, pessimistically, the level of unemployment in the age group might reach in 1978. The commission did not intend to provide for those who were out of work for only a few weeks, either on their initial entry into the labor market or transitionally later. In fact, it feared this might actually damage the employment prospects of the young people (MSC, 1977). In addition, early computer studies had convinced the

Holland working party that to include the short-term unemployed would push the total costs above politically acceptable levels. The 130,000 places provided in the program (as distinct from the annual maximum number of young people involved) would only be enough to cover the average number of those unemployed during the trough months at 1977 levels.

The commission, with powerful trade-union and management representation on both its working party and among the commissioners themselves, examined but rejected the possibility of restricting participation by imposing a compulsory waiting period or by denying early entry to those who chose to enter the labor market as soon as they had reached the legal school-leaving age instead of waiting until the end of the school year. However, the commission hoped to prevent the scheme from being swamped by the transitionally unemployed by stressing the role of the Careers Service in guiding applicants; and it also appeared that procedural delays in processing applications might serve effectively to screen out many of the short-term unemployed who insisted on their right to participate.

The commission estimated that the gross cost of its program for a full year would be £168.5 million (at 1976 prices) as compared with an existing commitment to spend £105 million on programs for the young in 1977–78. But it calculated that resulting savings in social security benefits and other expenditures would bring the net cost of the scheme down to around £95 million and suggested that there was "every prospect" that parts of the program would rank for aid from the European Social Fund. However, there was also some indication that the program might produce additional state expenditure outside its own costs. The commission noted that many of the opportunities proposed would be provided within educational establishments and that wherever possible the other opportunities would provide a "fully integrated element of further education" (MSC, 1977, p. 33). Future educational contributions, both within and beyond the Holland program, to alleviate problems of youth unemployment were being discussed between the government and the local authorities. The commission noted that difficulties might arise if those who wished to move from the program to

Figure 12. Proposals of the Manpower Services Commission for a program of opportunities for young people, by types of opportunities, Great Britain, 1977

Type of Opportunity	Title	Objective	Duration and Targets	Location	Provider	Progression
A. Courses to train and prepare young people for work	1. Assessment and employment induction courses	Improve employability by assessing work most suited for and interested in, improving knowledge of world of work and providing basic social skills.	Most 2 weeks A very few (Wider Opportunities Courses) up to 12 weeks	Skillcentres Colleges of Further Education but primarily employers' establishments.	TSA Local Education Authority Employers.	Some to normal employment. Most to basic skill course. A few to further education. Some to a work experience opportunity.
	2. Short industrial courses	Training for a specific though broad occupational area and employment at operator or semi-skilled level.	About 13 weeks Annual throughput 25,000	Skillcentres Colleges of Further Education Employers' establishments	TSA Local Education Authority Employers.	Many to normal employment. Some to further education. Others to a work experience opportunity.
	3. Remedial and preparatory courses	Reach basic levels of literacy and numeracy and basic entry requirements for other opportunities	As long as necessary for individual to achieve objective	Colleges of Further Education Special Schools Industrial and MSC premises Residential training colleges	Primarily Local Education Authority Some role for ESA and TSA	A few to normal employment. Most to other opportunities within Programme.
B. Work experience	4. Employers' premises	To give first hand experience of different kinds of work on employers'	On average 6 months Annual throughput 60,000	Employers' premises	Employers	Many to normal employment. Others to work preparation course or to further education.

Category	Programme	Objective	Duration / Throughput	Premises / Location	Sponsors	Destination
		ence of different kinds of work through the medium of projects	Annual throughput of 15,000		including local authorities, voluntary organizations etc.	to further education. Others to work preparation course.
	6. Training workshop	To give first hand experience of different kinds of work in a work group producing goods or services	Up to 12 months Annual throughput 10,000	Vacant factories and other premises or sites.	Sponsors as in 5 above	Many to normal employment. Some to further education. Others to work preparation course.
	7. Community service	To give first hand experience of different kinds of work through the medium of local community activities	Up to 12 months Annual throughput 15,000	Institutions (schools, hospitals, youth clubs, voluntary organizations) Specific community projects (health education services to housebound)	Social Services Voluntary organizations	Most to normal employment. Some to further education or work preparation course.
C. Community industry	8. Community industry	Provide help for seriously disadvantaged young people and those finding it hard to obtain and hold down jobs	On average 12 months Annual throughput 5,500	Local authority sponsored projects	Community industry working with local authorities	Most to normal employment. Some to work preparation course. A few to further education.
D. Incentive training grants	9. Premium grants training awards, etc	Meet anticipated requirements for manpower at higher skill levels	12 months or more Target 1977/78: 41,500	Employers' establishments, Colleges of Further Education, Industrial Training Board premises.	Industrial Training Boards and industry level bodies outside the Industrial Training Board's sector	All but a very few to normal employment.

Source: Manpower Services Commission (1977, p. 41).

Figure 13. **Proposals of the Manpower Service Commission for a new program of training courses and work experience**

	Assumed Average Duration	Places	Annual number of young people involved[a]	Cost (millior of £)
1. Work Preparation Courses				
a. Assessment or employment induction courses	2 weeks	3,000	60,000	8·3
b. Short industrial courses	3 months	8,000	25,000	22·5
c. Remedial or preparatory courses	26 weeks (max)	1,700 (approx.)	2,200	2·3
2. Work Experience				
a. Work experience on employers' premises	6 months	30,000	60,000	28·0
b. Project-based work experience	1 year	15,000	15,000	14·0
c. Training workshops	1 year	10,000	10,000	9·
d. Community service	1 year	15,000	15,000	14·0
e. Capital-contribution to (b)–(d) above	—	—	—	8·4
3. Additional Staff for Local Areas, etc.	—	—	—	2·0
TOTAL		82,700	187,200	109·
4. Other Programs				
a. Incentive training grants	1 year	41,500	41,500	46·
b. Community industry	1 year	5,500	5,500	12·
OVERALL TOTAL		129,700	234,200	168·

[a]These figures take account of some underoccupancy; since experience has shown that it is not possible for all courses to be full at all times.

Source: Manpower Services Commission (1977, p. 49).

full-time education were not eligible for the same allowance; the education service is reviewing this situation.

In spite of these considerations, the commission made it quite clear that the program must not be developed in isolation from other provisions for young people and from manpower policies as a whole. It must damage neither the incentive to be in full-time work or in full-time education, and it must help young people to develop vocationally relevant skills (which industry, in turn, must be encouraged to use) while meeting the personal needs of the youngsters. One paragraph in particular from the commission's report deserves to be quoted in full as exemplifying the philosophy and justification for the program:

> 3.6 A new programme should not stand apart from other programmes or policies for young people. Unemployed young people are not different from other young people except in the narrowest sense and in the shortest term. As they grow up and leave school or other forms of full-time education, the steps they have to take and the bridges they have to cross are the same as those their more fortunate friends and peers negotiate. Success or failure in getting a job is often a matter of luck and frequently determined by factors well beyond the control or achievement of the individual such as the state of the national economy, the local industrial structure, or the kind of preparation for work available at school. Unemployed young people are not failures: they are those whom others have so far failed. The kinds of needs unemployed young people have are essentially no different from the needs of others making the transition from full-time education to work, though those needs may sometimes be best met by different kinds of provision (MSC, 1977, p. 33).

It can be seen that the MSC proposals fall far short of the comprehensive scheme they had been invited to work out. They are deliberately pitched below the peak level of youth unemployment, trying to steer between the twin dangers of overkill and underprovision. If too many places are offered, some who would otherwise enter ordinary employment will be diverted into nonproductive work-experience schemes; if too few are offered, too many will remain jobless. The youth lobbies have criticized the scheme for providing too few places and suggested that what will follow will be a competition to get places, in which those whose prospects of ordinary employment are poorest will be the least successful. This is clearly an area of policy making where head and heart threaten to conflict, and the economist's quest for productive efficiency may clash with the social worker's concern for individual welfare. The resulting compromise is unlikely to satisfy either, but the cost of a fully comprehensive scheme, even if it were deemed to make economic sense, would be prohibitive.

Intervention in the Labor Market for Those Aged 19 to 25

Those aged 19 or over were the principal beneficiaries of the two major short-term unemployment countermeasures, the Job Creation Program and the TOPS training scheme. Job creation as a short-term measure was due to end in the summer of 1977, while TOPS changed its pace, subordinating its earlier priority of expansion to relieve pressure in the labor market to a concentration on quality, which would mean a more selective and smaller program. Although the government could simply refund the existing JCP for a further period, as it had done in the past, the MSC advised that, with the removal of those under age 19 into the Holland program, the opportunity should be taken to refine the JCP and turn it into a longer-term program aimed principally at those 19 to 25. The discussions that took place between the government and the commission over the Holland report included this question of a successor program to the JCP.

The youth organizations, in particular a body called Youthaid—a lobby formed by the British Youth Council and the National Youth Bureau (together with some of their respective member organizations), the National Association of Youth Clubs, and Community Service Volunteers—urged that the government fund on a much larger scale the employment of youth over the age of 19 in community service and youth work. In fact, the Holland working party, although it did not make this clear in its report, envisaged that many of the 8,000 adults whom it estimated would be required to lead its work-experience projects would be drawn from those aged 19 to 25. But Youthaid and the British Youth Council went a good deal further in their prescription for intervention in the youth labor market as a whole. They continued to urge that the government adopt a manpower strategy separate from its industrial strategy that would include deliberate investment in labor-intensive projects as a means of offsetting the increasing degree of structural youth unemployment, which they saw as unavoidable in any mainstream progress toward greater productivity.

6

Social and Cultural
Changes in the
Status of Youth

Much has been written about the development of a youth culture in the period since World War II. By the middle 1950s, the combination of increased affluence and energetic commercial activities to exploit it had focused attention on the tastes, aspirations, and consumption patterns of those 15 to 25 years of age. People began to talk of a new teenage/young-adult culture, bridging social classes and linking life-styles through the language of popular music and fashions. Staying on at school became a less exclusive mark of social or intellectual elitism; but at the same time expansion of further and higher education and the expectation that it would become part of the social initiation process for an increasing section of the community helped to formalize the prolongation of adolescence. Young people found themselves pulled in different directions: better diet and more affluence brought earlier physical maturity; changing social conventions brought more freedom and independence of parental control. Yet the extension of education and the sophistication of skills required by a complex industrial society lengthened the period of transition between childhood and adulthood for an increasing proportion of the population. A commercial, classless, youthful image emerged, based on the spending habits of employed young men and women. Yet for the growing minority who continued in education, the artificially extended adolescence was a time of relative poverty and low living standards. For them, economic gratification, which had traditionally been associated with middle-class social values as access to extended education was enlarged, was postponed, leading to rejection of middle-class values, to doubts that the pay-off would justify the sacrifice, or at least to resentment of the prolonged period of preparation required before enjoying the fruits of study and training.

One consequence of these developments was the growth of a self-conscious notion of the "student" and of a student class and student solidarity. This notion has gained only limited support in Britain, where student politics have largely been the preserve of a small minority of the politically active. These have included several constantly regrouping left-wing radical groups, with the Communists clearly recognizable to the right of most of the Marxist elements, while in the last two or three years groups affiliated to the Conservative Party student organization have made considerable progress, both at the level of individual universities and colleges and in the National Union of Students, where a broad left-wing coalition of Communist and other socialist groups dominates. It should be noted, however, that the electoral processes of student politics are ideally suited to produce undemocratic results, and the great majority of student opinion is much less radical and more apathetic than the contentious proceedings of the National Union of Students might suggest.

Sociologists have studied the development of the youth culture in depth, with special attention to the *rites de passage* by which the young pass from youth to adulthood. In Britain, alongside the new social phenomena connected with fashions and pop music and the outward signs of a distinctive life-style, there came and went a sequence of sociopolitical movements that attracted support from young people. There were the Teddy Boys and the Mods and Rockers, the men who wore their hair short and the men who wore their hair long, and the successful revolt against formal styles of clothing; but there was also the participation of young people in the Campaign for Nuclear Disarmament in the early 1960s and later in a welter of radical political movements and a more generalized indignation against environmental pollution. By the time the age groups born in the "baby boom" years just after World War II reached the university in the later 1960s, the student revolution had begun, and sociologists were presented with a rich selection of case studies from Berkeley to Berlin, Tokyo to Paris and Rome, the London School of Economics to the University of Essex.

Looking at the scene in the late 1970s, it becomes evident that the youth revolution was only a particular manifestation of a much larger revolution affecting society as a whole. The student revolt in Britain was always a pretty pallid affair; not only was the student community extremely small, it was also highly privileged and well looked after. Very few of the grievances that aroused the university student in Germany or France in 1968 were available to student militants in Britain, who had to be content with campaigning for more participation in academic decision making and against petty rules. As the universities themselves had lost confidence in petty rules and were prepared to accept student membership on university committees (on terms that in practice left the academics with effective safeguards), the necessary adjustments were made with relative ease.

Much more significant than the student revolt, or any other of the changes forced on society by disenchanted young people, were the larger social changes not specially related to young people but which greatly affected the world in which they were growing up. Within the space of a few years during the 1960s, Britain saw the abolition of the death penalty for murder; changes in the abortion, divorce, and homosexuality laws; new gaming laws; and the lowering of the age of majority (and the voting age) to 18. Having lived for many years with fairly conservative conventions about what could and could not be represented on screen and stage, Britain dismantled a centuries-old system of theater censorship and applied new liberal laws to obscenity in books and magazines. The "permissive society" materialized during the 1960s, and it became popular to talk of "swinging London." And with all this came a general loosening of family relationships and the abdication of discipline over children by many parents who saw the permissive society, in part at least, as removing from them responsibility for their children's behavior. In a different but no less forceful way, the use of contraceptive pills compounded the new freedom in sexual relationships and, with easier, legal abortion, modified relationships between young people. Many of these changes have diminished the influence of families over the behavior of children and increased the influence of peer groups and the commercial media.

During the 1960s, the proportion of mothers doing paid work outside the home increased by more than 70 percent. In 1971, 49 percent of the female population was classified as economically active, including 49.2 percent of the 18-to-24 age group and 56.7 percent of those 25 to 44. Also in 1971, there were an estimated 620,000 one-parent families with 1,080,000 children—10 percent of all households with dependent children. This group has grown steadily with easier divorce legislation and the rise in the number of divorces through the 1960s and 1970s. The present number is about 125,000 per year (double the 1970 figure) which compares with about 420,000 marriages. Alongside these developments has been the progress of the women's movement and the enactment of a Sex Discrimination Act in 1975 with very wide application. It remains to be seen how effective the legal remedies offered to women who are discriminated against will be, but this movement represents a major piece of public education indicating an important shift in public policy that is already modifying individual and corporate behavior.

There is room for endless argument on whether the generation gap has gotten wider or narrower or remained the same. If the changes affecting young people are themselves part of a social change affecting the community as a whole, there is reason to doubt that the generation gap has widened. For every item of evidence suggesting that young people are alienated and disenchanted, there are dozens more that show them fitting into the present society and accepting its competitive disciplines. The "dropout" emerged during the 1960s as a social phenomenon, worrying middle-class parents and associated with various forms of academic failure or the rejection of academic objectives. The practice of students "stopping off" for a year or so to go to Khatmandu or work on a building site became common in a period when it was still relatively easy for students to get well-paid, short-term employment. Even so, the great majority of university students continued to take the normal three-year degree course and to get suitable employment at the end. Graduate unemployment has not risen to serious proportions, though the length of time new graduates have had to wait before getting jobs has lengthened and shortened with the state of the economy, and, in anticipation of harder employment conditions, there has been a retreat from the less vocationally useful subjects in higher education and a rise in the number of would-be doctors, lawyers, accountants, and engineers. One consequence of the relatively low participation rate in post-secondary education is that those who find themselves in this sector of education in Britain have been less adversely affected in time of economic recession than they would have been had they been more numerous.

Therefore, while it is right to study forms of behavior among young people that can be taken as an index of alienation, it is well to begin by noting that conformity is more typical of youthful attitudes than rebellion or dissent. Professor John Egglestone of the University of Keele, author of a recent study of youth policy for the Department of Education and Science (1975), had occasion to draw attention to this.

> Our evidence does not support the sophisticated radicalism of young people, often assumed to exist by many writers on the "youth scene." . . . Whilst there is unquestionably a strong desire to "change society" in fundamental ways among some young people, our evidence suggests that this is not a majority view. It is confined to a politically conscious minority. It is more often held by adult workers, particularly in community action projects, than by members.

The majority of members are well aware of the nature of contemporary society, and disposed to accept it. Most are content to find a meaningful place within it that provides a satisfying self-image; to be able to make decisions within the present society rather than refashion it. It is this that we mean by "counting for something." Indeed our evidence showed there was a widespread respect for structure, ordered relationships, and a stable framework of social organisation. The most radical position of the average member seemed to be the desire for some sort of redistribution of power by which he and others could share more readily in a largely unchanged society. (Often he may not wish to exercise power, only to know he could if he wished.)

Crime

The difficulties of making comparison from one year to another based on the criminal statistics are well-known: the definitions of criminal behavior change; so do the practices of the police and of the courts. Nevertheless, there is little doubt that crime among young people has risen steadily in recent years and that this rise in juvenile crime is steeper than the rise in crime throughout society. A third of all those found guilty of, or formally cautioned for, indictable offenses in 1975 were under age 17. Over 17 percent of the 14 to 18 age group were convicted or cautioned for indictable offenses in 1975; with all the qualifications that have to be made about comparisons, this was twice the juvenile crime rate a decade earlier. Crime among the 14- to 18-year-olds had doubled, while the increase for the community as a whole was only 70 percent.

Women and girls are between five and six times more law abiding (or more successful in evading discovery). Among both men and women there is a marked fall-off in the crime rate with age: young men aged 17 to 20 are 11 times as likely to appear in conviction statistics as those aged 30 and over; in the case of women, the equivalent ratio is about 5 to 1.

This growth of juvenile crime is linked in the minds of most commentators with social alienation. "There is little doubt," according to Professor F. H. McClintock, professor of criminology at the University of Edinburgh, "that part of our problem involving young people is the result of alienation from a social system created primarily by the adult population" (McClintock, 1974, pp. 5–6). He continues:

> A sense of apathy and alienation probably lies behind the criminal violence in schools and the growth of truancy. Also the repetitive and uninteresting jobs of many youths in industrial employment could be so lacking in satisfaction as to turn them to seek an outlet for their boredom in criminal excitement in a monotonous urban environment during leisure periods. A final point which ought to be made is that, although we are focusing attention on the criminality of youth, it has to be stressed that the vast majority of youth in this country never come into direct conflict with the law enforcement processes or get charged with criminal offences. Although the age groups that I am concerned with have much higher conviction rates than the adult population, and though such rates have been increasing in recent years, still no more than 6 young people are involved per annum for every 100 in the male population. While elsewhere I have indicated, by the use of a projection model, that only 20 percent of the male population and 3 percent of the female population will be recorded as involved in a crime of any sort between the ages of 10 and 20 years, the chances of a young male becoming a youthful recidivist is less than 4 percent. The vast majority of young people are never convicted of crime; of those that are involved in crime the majority have only one or two skirmishes with the law, but rarely do such skirmishes extend to criminal violence. The often-made assertion that the younger generation is identified as both criminal and violent, when examined carefully in relation to crime data in police returns and the demographic data on the population, is found to be a public myth.

However, to make such a statement is not to deny that in Great Britain today there is a serious crime problem or to deny the continuous annual increase in the volume of violent crime recorded by the police. In England and Wales serious violent crime and robbery with violence increased from 17,000 in 1960 to 69,000 in 1973. In Scotland the corresponding increase was from 2,000 in 1960 to 5,000 in 1973. The increase in recorded violence during the last thirteen years was therefore 288 percent in England and Wales and 173 percent in Scotland.

Whatever the causes, the trend is getting worse, and many of the problems of the inner city on which youthful crime thrives are getting worse, too. A study by the Community Relations Commission looked at the linked problems of unemployment and homelessness and the existence of a small but recognizable group of young people from both majority and minority groups who drift into petty crime, prostitution, and join others supporting themselves after a fashion by hustling. While there are municipal social service agencies and voluntary organizations that theoretically provide welfare services to young people, the national and local resources devoted to them are inadequate to cope with the potential demand, and, in any case, many of those in need of help are reluctant to accept it from official sources.

Drug Abuse

In the area of illegal drugs, statistics are again notoriously imperfect. The number of registered addicts shows a trend which, on the face of it, might seem modestly encouraging (Table 23). The number of registered addicts in the under-25 age groups in 1975 was 600, compared with 773 in 1970. But the general view is that the figures grossly understate the extent of the problem and that there is currently an increase in hard-drug use that has begun to show up in the criminal statistics. The 1976 report of the Standing Conference on Drug Abuse also drew attention to the increasing number of "multiple drug

Table 23. **Dangerous drugs: numbers of registered addicts,**
United Kingdom, 1970 to 1975

	1970	*1971*	*1972*	*1973*	*1974*	*1975*
Number registered as taking drugs on 31 December[a]:	1,426	1,549	1,615	1,815	1,972	1,954
Males	1,051	1,133	1,194	1,369	1,459	1,438
Females	375	416	421	446	513	516
Age distribution:						
Under 20 years	142	118	96	84	64	39
20 and under 25	631	722	727	750	692	561
25 and under 30	237	288	376	530	684	754
30 and under 35	90	112	117	134	163	219
35 and under 50	112	112	118	136	163	169
50 and over	195	177	165	180	198	194
Age not stated	19	20	16	1	8	18
Type of drug[b]:						
Methadone	991	1,160	1,278	1,439	1,552	1,543
Heroin	437	385	338	378	392	316
Morphine	105	100	89	83	82	70
Pethidine	77	70	59	50	61	62
Cocaine	57	58	46	51	47	23
Dipipanone	45	49	37	48	76	133
Dextromoramide	28	35	32	49	64	70
Other drugs	13	9	7	8	11	7

[a] Comparable figures for years before 1970 are not available.

[b] Addicts who are receiving more than one drug are shown against each drug they receive. Heroin and methadone are the drugs most commonly used together. In 1970, 254 addicts were receiving both drugs: the figures for 1971, 1972, 1973, 1974, and 1975 are 229, 201, 223, 243, and 212 respectively.

Note: In 1975 there were 36 hospitals holding special clinics for the out-patient treatment of drug dependence, all having access in-patient facilities. Treatment is also provided in general psychiatric units.

Source: Central Statistical Office, 1976.

misusers who engage in the indiscriminate and highly dangerous use of a wide range of drugs including alcohol and barbituates. Many are homeless and rootless, frequently overdose and are repeatedly admitted to casualty wards, some several times a day. . . . They lack any common identity with narcotic drug takers, appearing to be lonely, isolated and often very disturbed young people. With hindsight it would appear that the official perception of the drug problem in the mid-1960s was unduly narrow and probably distorted by the hysteria surrounding heroin addiction at that time" (Standing Conference on Drug Abuse, 1976, p. 3).

While the total annual number of criminal convictions for drug offenses of all kinds was about 14,000 in 1975, the number of offenses relating to cannabis is going down and those concerned with more dangerous drugs is going up. However, this is not necessarily a clear guide to actual behavior. It is generally supposed that soft drugs are relatively widely used, but that they have ceased to enjoy high status as evidence of a social problem. Schools and colleges are now much less concerned about cannabis; the consumption of alcohol has replaced cannabis as the headmaster's worry at boarding schools, but there is no reason to suppose that the use of cannabis has actually declined.

Alcohol

There has been a marked rise in the number of admissions to mental hospitals and units of men and women diagnosed as suffering from alcoholism or alcoholic psychosis (Figure 14). Since the middle of 1960s, the per-capita consumption of alcohol has increased by 30 percent, by far the biggest increase being in wines and, to a lesser extent, spirits. (Even so, both beer and spirits consumption [22 gallons and 0.8 gallons respectively] was well below the pre-1914 level). Young people are among the heaviest spenders on alcohol and therefore likely to be among those most likely to suffer from its excessive use. The Family Expenditure Survey (1973) shows that those in the 16 to 19 age group spend 92 percent of the average expenditure on alcohol by all persons aged 16 and over. Those aged 20 to 24 spend 156 percent of the average. In both cases males spend considerably more than females.

Britain can be seen as moving toward a new pattern of social provision for the older teenagers—that is, for those between the end of compulsory education and the official age of majority.

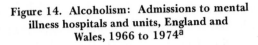

Figure 14. Alcoholism: Admissions to mental
illness hospitals and units, England and
Wales, 1966 to 1974[a]

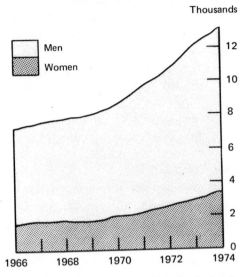

[a]Figures are for hospitals and units under Regional
Hospital Boards and teaching hospitals. They include
patients whose first or second diagnosis was
alcoholism or alcoholic psychosis.

Source: Department of Health and Social Security.

But it is not easy to see in current developments any substantial
change in employment, education, and training for the 18-to-24
age group except on the basis of the gradual evolution of the
present arrangements. As has been suggested, the lines of possible development in postsecondary education are visible, but in
the late 1970s there is not much evidence of public support for
forward movement along these lines. At the 16-to-19 age level,
however, there are many more signs of movement and evidence
of willingness on the part of the politicians to back ad hoc
arrangements to alleviate the effects of youth unemployment.
These arrangements will, of themselves, generate system changes
that could be far reaching.

The MSC proposals of 1977 (Figure 13), while presented
cautiously as countercyclical measures aimed primarily at con-

taining the rise in youth unemployment, can be seen in this light. These proposals fit into the philosophical framework of a "youth opportunity guarantee." If this philosophy prevails, it will not be possible in the long run to offer such a guarantee to a strictly limited number of young people without extending it to all. What will emerge will add up to a system of vocational preparation, a series of organized experiences combining work experience with learning. Many things will follow from this. A local and regional structure will come into being to administer the scheme. This will operate alongside (but separate from) the system of local government that administers upper secondary schools and further education. The MSC schemes will be financed directly from national funds and, while particular projects will be developed on a decentralized basis by local groups, the central direction of the plan will be in the hands of the MSC. The educational system, on the other hand, lacks such clear-cut central direction, because the powers of the secretary of state are strictly limited by law, and in many respects coordinated action depends on persuasion and negotiated compromise.

If a system of vocational preparation through work experience and related schemes comes into existence parallel to the education system, there are soon going to be problems of selection: Who is going to be admitted to which project on the basis of what criteria? The schemes themselves will come to form part of the social selection mechanism. Until now, the Training Services Agency (the MSC's training arm) has selected candidates for its training projects on the time-honored basis of judging their capacity to benefit: the "likeliest lads" have been those most readily taken on. If the MSC proposals (and the £18 a week for all successful applicants) offer fewer places than there are potential candidates, will the criteria for admission still favor those most likely to do well? If so, the scheme is liable to mop up many who would otherwise be well placed to get jobs anyway and exclude many of those whose poor job prospects have helped to launch the scheme. However, to discriminate in favor of those least likely to do well would also raise problems.

Reference has already been made to the difficulties that a large-scale development of work-experience schemes could present to the education system. If the MSC schemes develop with a substantial element of training and vocational education, there will be direct competition for the allegiance of many young people between the full-time school and further-education system on the one hand and the MSC schemes on the other: the MSC schemes will pay out £18 a week to their chosen candidates and the secondary system nothing to theirs, except insofar as they may be eligible for education maintenance allowances. These latter allowances (EMAs) are at present heavily dependent on the discretion of individual local education authorities. Where paid at all, they average little more than £2 a week, and they are only paid to the poorest families. Inevitably—and rightly—the British government has blanched at the idea of subsidizing all young people to stay on at school when already, without any allowances, so many do so voluntarily, supported by their parents and their own weekend earnings. But the MSC proposals have brought EMAs back into the public discussion, and in so doing have highlighted the inadequately considered side effects that the MSC proposals will bring with them.

A logical development would be a new administrative link between the local-authority network of upper secondary schools and further education and the MSC's network of industrial training. But this is not easy to achieve. The philosophy and raison d'être of the education service is very different from that of the MSC; so are the vested interests concerned.

A take-over of training by the education system is a fantasy occasionally indulged in by empire-building teacher-trade-unionists, but not only is such a take-over improbable in the extreme, it would also give the educators a responsibility they could not carry out. Likewise, a take-over of a large part of post-age-16 school and further education, though another fantasy entertained by those who have been beguiled by the aggressive style (and long purse) of the MSC, is not within the bounds of probability and would certainly not be desirable. But it is clear that, on the educational side, there is some reason to think that the industrial and commercial point of view should be more strongly stated, and, if through the Holland proposals the MSC is going to be drawn more and more into this field, some new and formal mechanism to manage this is going to be required, especially if more experience of work and industry is to be offered to pupils before they reach the end of compulsory schooling.

If ordinary jobs for young people in industry, commerce, and the public services do continue to become more scarce and an increasing proportion of the age group remain in school, further education, or structured forms of work experience and vocational preparation, there will have to be a spectrum of opportunities for all, stretching from the traditional pursuit of formal academic education at one end to work experience with minimal training or education at the other. To achieve this there would have to be a determined attempt to reduce the artificial barriers that now constrain the schools and colleges and that in the short-term (if the MSC proposals for cash allowances are fully implemented) will likely be raised rather than lowered. With more part-time education, more passage in and out of school and in and out of work experience, the case for a new and essentially more adventurous approach to recurrent education is strong.

These speculations may well arouse skepticism. It is much easier to write of obstacles in the way of this kind of development than to express confidence that it will come about. The legal and institutional hurdles are formidable and would only be cleared by a government very determined and very clear about its aims and not required to modify every move to respond to immediate pressures. The structure of educational administration is tied up with the whole structure of local government. Local government has recently been reorganized (in 1973) at the cost of great political pain and grief. No political party will readily embark again on local government reform in a hurry. But there are signs that, within five years, there could be a major review of educational administration (brought forward, in part, by weaknesses in the present system). If this were so, many doors might open; the need for new patterns of organization for the 16 to 19 age group would be one of the pressures behind any new education law.

The potential cost of any major extension of the youth opportunity guarantee for the 16-to-19 age group is the most obvious deterrent to action and the most obvious reason why politicians prefer to wait and see what happens rather than make ambitious plans and drive them through against fierce opposition. Doubts about the nature of youth unemployment and the reasons behind its increase will also counsel caution. One reason why there is now a need to find ways of increasing the range of options for young people is that their prospects have been relatively worsened by the unforeseen side effects of other well-intentioned social policies. Behind any argument about how youth opportunities can be improved is a larger argument about the desirability of further large-scale public intervention in the labor market and the uncertainties surrounding the outcomes of most projected policies. The political sensitivity that attends the monthly publication of the unemployment figures has the effect of concentrating attention on the input of labor into the economy. If this were to divert attention from the output of the economy, it could do a disservice all around. A distinguishing characteristic of the British economy is low productivity. Common prudence suggests that any design for improving the induction of young people from dependence to independence, from school to work, must have in view improving productivity and increasing the wealth available at the end to pay for the material aspects of the good life which, in a democracy, is not to be prescribed by platonic guardians, but by the individual choice of voting citizens. Of course, fundamental questions about growth and its limits present themselves with increasing persistence. But so far no major political party in Britain has responded to the romantic appeal of the zero-growth economy. It would obviously have enormous impact on the whole question of employment, not just the employment of young people, and introduce into the discussion a wider range of intractable issues which could not be considered seriously without an entirely different conceptual framework.

References

Association of University Teachers (AUT). *University Student Numbers.* London: United House, April 1977.

British Youth Council. *Youth Unemployment: Causes and Cures.* Report of a Working Party. London: British Youth Council, March 1977.

Central Advisory Council for Education. *Report on Early Leaving.* London: Her Majesty's Stationery Office, 1954.

Central Advisory Council for Education. *Education Between the Ages of 15 and 18* (the Crowther Report). London: Her Majesty's Stationery Office, 1960.

Central Policy Review Staff. *Population and Social Services.* London: Her Majesty's Stationery Office, 1977.

Central Statistical Office. *Annual Abstract of Statistics.* London: Her Majesty's Stationery Office, various years.

Central Statistical Office. *Social Trends 1976.* London: Her Majesty's Stationery Office, 1976.

Central Statistical Office. *Economic Trends.* London: Her Majesty's Stationery Office, February 1977.

Community Relations Commission (CRC). *Between Two Cultures.* London: Elliot House, 1976.

Department of Education and Science (DES). *Education: A Framework for Expansion.* London: Her Majesty's Stationery Office, 1972.

Department of Education and Science. *Careers Education in Secondary Schools.* London: Her Majesty's Stationery Office, 1973.

Department of Education and Science. *Public Expenditure to 1978-79.* London: Her Majesty's Stationery Office, January 1975.

Department of Education and Science. *Education Statistics for the United Kingdom 1974.* London: Her Majesty's Stationery Office, 1976a.

Department of Education and Science. *Statistics of Education.* London: Her Majesty's Stationery Office, 1974 (various volumes) 1976b.

Department of Education and Science. *Higher Education into the 1990s: A Discussion Document.* London: Elizabeth House, February 1978.

Department of Employment (DE). *Family Expenditure Survey.* London: Her Majesty's Stationery Office, annual.

Department of Employment. *New Earnings Survey.* London: Her Majesty's Stationery Office, 1968, 1970, 1971, 1972, 1973, 1974, 1975, 1976.

Department of Employment. *Unqualified, Untrained and Unemployed: Report of a Working Party Set Up by the National Youth Employment Council.* London: Her Majesty's Stationery Office, 1974.

Department of Employment. *British Labour Statistics Yearbook 1974.* London: Her Majesty's Stationery Office, 1976.

Department of Employment *Gazette.* "New Projections of Future Labour Force." June 1977, pp. 587–592.

Department of Employment *Gazette.* "Unemployment Rates by Age." July 1977, pp. 718–719.

Department of Employment *Gazette.* "Young People Entering Employment in 1974." December 1975, pp. 1269-1273.

Department of Health and Social Security Leaflets N112, SB9. London: Department of Health and Social Security.

Eastwood, G. *Skilled Labour Shortages in the United Kingdom with Particular Reference to the Engineering Industry.* London: British North American Committee, 1976.

Egglestone, J. "Values for Youth." *New Society,* January 18, 1975, p. 129.

Engineering Industries Training Board (EITB). *The Craftsman in Engineering: An Interim Report.* London: EITB, 1975.

Floud, J. "The Educational Experience of the Adult Population of England and Wales as at July 1949." In D. V. Glass (Ed.), *Social Mobility in Britain.* London: Routledge and Kegan Paul, 1954, pp. 98–140.

Glass, D. V. (Ed.). *Social Mobility in Britain.* London: Routledge and Kegan Paul, 1954.

Lomas, G. *The Inner City: A Preliminary Investigation of the Dynamics of Current Labour and Housing Markets with Specific Reference to Minority Groups in Inner London.* London: London Council of Social Service, 1975.

London *Times,* Nov. 15, 1976.

Manpower Services Commission (MSC). *Vocational Preparation for Young People.* London: Selkirk House, 1975.

Manpower Services Commission. *Towards a Comprehensive Manpower Policy.* London: Her Majesty's Stationery Office, 1976.

Manpower Services Commission. *Young People at Work: Report of a Working Party of the MSC.* London: Her Majesty's Stationery Office, 1977.

Manpower Services Commission/Department of Employment (MSC-DE). *Training for Vital Skills: A Consultative Document.* London: Her Majesty's Stationery Office, 1976.

Manpower Services Commission/Department of Employment. *Joint Memorandum on the Job Creation Programme: Evidence to the Social Services and Employment Sub-Committee of the House of Commons Expenditure Committee.* January 24, 1977, mimeo.

McClintock, F. H. *Youth and Violence.* Paper presented to the Edinburgh branch of the Institute for the Study and Treatment of Delinquency, University of Edinburgh, 1974, mimeo.

McIntosh, N. S., Calder, J. A., and Swift, B. *A Degree of Difference.* Guildford, Surrey: Society for Research into Higher Education at the University of Surrey, September 1976.

Metcalfe, D. *Youth Unemployment in Britain.* Paper presented to the Ditchley Foundation Conference on Youth. Oxfordshire, Ditchley Park, 1976.

National Institute for Economic and Social Research (NIESR). *Quarterly Economic Review,* February 1977.

Office of Population, Censuses and Surveys. *Census of Population.* London: Her Majesty's Stationery Office, 1961, 1966, 1971.

Office of Population, Censuses and Surveys (OPCS). *General Household Survey.* London: Her Majesty's Stationery Office, 1971–1974.

Office of Population, Censuses and Surveys. *Population Trends 7.* London: Her Majesty's Stationery Office, 1977.

Office of Population, Censuses and Surveys. *Population Projections 1974-2014.* London: Her Majesty's Stationery Office, 1976.

Report of the Committee of Higher Education (The Robbins Report). London: Her Majesty's Stationery Office, 1963.

Society of Education Officers (SEO). *Comment on "Preparation for Working Life and for Transition from Education to Work," EEC Education Action Programme.* London: London College of Printing, 1977.

Smith, Sir Alex. *Wisdom Lost in Knowledge.* Bolland Memorial Lecture. Bristol Polytechnic, March 1976, mimeo.

Standing Conference on Drug Abuse (SCODA). *Annual Report 1975–76.* London: Standing Conference on Drug Abuse, 1976.

Universities Central Council on Admissions. *Statistic Supplement to the Annual Report 1967-68 and 1973-74.* Cheltenham, Gloucestershire: Universities Central Council on Admissions.

Worswick, G. D. N. (Ed.). *The Concept and Measurement of Involuntary Unemployment.* London: George Allen & Unwin for the Royal Economic Society, 1976.